Advertising Measurement and Decision Making

MARKETING SCIENCE INSTITUTE
SERIES OF BOOKS

PUBLISHED WITH ALLYN AND BACON, INC.

Advertising Measurement and Decision Making (1968)
Brand Policy Determination (1967)
Comparative Analysis for International Marketing (1967)
Experiments on the Value of Information in Simulated Market-
    ing Environments (1967)
Industrial Buying and Creative Marketing (1967)
Personal Selling in a Modern Perspective (1967)
Promotional Decisions Using Mathematical Models (1967)

OTHER PUBLICATIONS

Marketing Development in the European Economic Community
    (1964)
Promotional Decision Making: Practice and Theory (1964)
The Meaning and Sources of Marketing Theory (1965)
Marketing Education in the United States (1964)

MARKETING SCIENCE INSTITUTE

3401 Market Street
Philadelphia, Pa.   19104

THE MARKETING SCIENCE INSTITUTE was established in 1962 in Philadelphia for the purpose of conducting the kinds of basic research that would serve to advance the productivity and efficiency of marketing. The Institute's research and educational activity is designed to (1) contribute to the emergence of a science of marketing, and (2) stimulate increased application of scientific techniques to the understanding and solving of marketing problems.

Financial support for MSI is provided by leading business firms. In addition, the personnel of these firms contribute generously of their time and ability as members of MSI committees, study groups, and as advisors and consultants on MSI research projects and reports.

All research reports and findings of the Marketing Science Institute are made generally available through publication. In compliance with MSI policy, publication of this report has been approved by a majority of the Board of Trustees.

MARKETING SCIENCE INSTITUTE

ADVERTISING MEASUREMENT
AND DECISION MAKING

Edited and Directed by

PATRICK J. ROBINSON
Research Director
Marketing Science Institute

By

HOMER M. DALBEY
Economist
Bank of America

IRWIN GROSS
Assistant Professor
Wharton School of Finance and Commerce
University of Pennsylvania

and

YORAM WIND
Assistant Professor
Wharton School of Finance and Commerce
University of Pennsylvania

Allyn & Bacon, Inc.
Boston

Preface

IF YOU ARE a business executive involved in any way making advertising decisions, you can benefit from this book. It will be of help to you in deciding whether your advertising resources are being used most efficiently; and there are some implications as to whether your advertising program is satisfactorily integrated with other aspects of your company's total marketing activities.

If you are a research executive you will find in this book some ideas for evaluating existing techniques and procedures that attempt to measure advertising effectiveness. The type of analysis will be of help to you in considering the pros and cons of various approaches.

If you are a teacher or student of marketing, you will find some new insights into the complex question of advertising measurement. You will also obtain some new insights into the decision making process.

ADVERTISING MEASUREMENT AND DECISION MAKING is an example of the application of scientific methods in defining and solving a practical marketing problem. It is a direct outgrowth of two earlier Marketing Science Institute exploratory projects; and it also reflects the type of investigation reported in 1964 in the book PROMOTIONAL DECISION MAKING: PRACTICE AND THEORY, by Patrick J. Robinson and David J. Luck.

The wide variety of methods used in attempting to pretest, posttest, and otherwise measure various aspects of advertising are a considerable source of confusion for a good many people in marketing. This confusion results in part from the lack of a uniform standard of comparison for the various measurement techniques. It is also due to lack of understanding of the assumptions underlying the various techniques.

The main purpose of the present book has been to develop an analytical device to aid advertisers both in the *comprehension* and *selection* of techniques related to the measurement of various aspects of advertising effectiveness. The eventual result was the

xi

development of an *Idealized Measurement Procedure*, which can be called *IMP*. Although this IMP does not really exist, it can be extremely useful as a standard against which to contrast various measuring techniques. It is an *ideal* or perfect standard for measuring advertising effectiveness.

Two orientations influenced the development of the IMP framework. The first was the view that decision making in advertising can be improved through better understanding of the techniques designed to measure advertising effectiveness. Second, there is a practical and operational orientation, including a sharp distinction between decision making and effectiveness of advertising.

These basic ideas are developed in Chapter I, along with some definitions used in this book. Various performance measures and related issues concerning the so-called hierarchy of effects, and an alternative to it, are dealt with in Chapter II.

Against this background the IMP framework is developed in Chapter III, with its seven basic elements examined in detail. These same elements are considered likewise with relation to controlled market tests, split-run tests, on-air tests, and various other techniques. The assumptions underlying the various techniques are analyzed in Chapters IV and V according to their possible acceptability to users.

Even further implications of the IMP system are described in Chapter VI, and a supplementary evaluation procedure. This leads to the summary and conclusions of Chapter VII.

ACKNOWLEDGMENTS

The present work was initiated by Michael H. Halbert, Technical Director of the Marketing Science Institute, who supervised its early stages and offered many helpful ideas. Albert W. Frey, Dean of the Graduate School of Business Administration, University of Pittsburgh, also made significant contributions in the early stages of the study. Thanks are also due Albert B. Richardson, Vice President, Chesebrough-Pond's Inc. for his constructive criticism of earlier drafts of this study. A number of his suggestions are reflected in this book.

Others whose aid is gratefully acknowledged include: Donald Burkett and Kelley Clowe, formerly graduate students at the Wharton School of Finance and Commerce, University of Pennsylvania; Charles L. Hinkle, Professor of Marketing, University of Colorado; Laurence W. Jacobs, Assistant Professor of Marketing, University of Hawaii; and Thomas T. Semon, Marketing Consultant, New York.

The efficient assistance of Mrs. Patricia Coffey, Research Assistant of the Marketing Science Institute, who helped in organizing the final draft of this book, is appreciated.

Thanks are also due to the executives of those firms who in the early stages of the present investigation supplied information about their own experiences with respect to advertising measurement and decision making.

Finally, and most important, this book is really the result of the combined work of the three authors—Homer M. Dalbey, Irwin Gross, and Yoram Wind—whose individual contributions I have attempted to blend into a coordinated report to advertising management.

PATRICK J. ROBINSON
Director of Management Studies and
Member of the Operating Committee
Marketing Science Institute

Contents

PREFACE   xi

HIGHLIGHTS OF THIS BOOK   xix

Chapter

I MEASUREMENT FOR ADVERTISING DECISIONS   1

Can Advertising Performance Be Measured?   2

What Are We Measuring?   4

Measurement and the Major Advertising Decisions   6

How can Advertising Performance Be Measured?   10

The Dilemma of Advertising Effectiveness   13

II MEASURES OF PERFORMANCE   17

Absolute Versus Relative Effectiveness   17

Some Typical Advertising Effects   18

Hierarchy of Effects   20

Correlates of Effects   23

Some Implications   25

xv

III   COMPARISON OF IDEALIZED MEASUREMENT PROCEDURE
      WITH OTHER TECHNIQUES   26

      Syndicated Techniques   27

      Nonsyndicated Techniques   34

      The Seven Basic Attributes of Measurement Techniques   38

      Some Implications   45

IV   ASSUMPTIONS CONCERNING THE SCOPE OF ADVERTISING
     AND RESPONSES MEASURED   47

      Conditions of Acceptability   48

      The Basic Assumptions   50

      Some Implications   70

V   ASSUMPTIONS CONCERNING THE ENVIRONMENTAL
    FACTORS   71

      Further Basic Assumptions   71

      Some Implications   79

VI   APPLICATIONS OF IMP IN ANALYZING MEASUREMENT
     TECHNIQUES   81

      Advertising Measurement for Advertising Management   82

      Validating the Measurement Techniques   84

      Some Implications   89

VII   SOME CONCLUSIONS   90

      Information for Advertising Decisions   90

      Evaluating Alternative Advertising Measurement
      Techniques   91

The Meaning of "Advertising Effectiveness"   92

Final Considerations   93

FOOTNOTES   94

INDEX   98

Highlights
of This Book

THE POSSIBILITY OF MEASURING advertising is an appealing idea, but measurement poses complex problems.

This book on *Advertising Measurement and Decision Making* suggests a systematic approach to many of these problems. Although no easy answers are offered, the authors do show what steps need to be taken to decide on the applicability of various techniques of advertising measurement.

The book will be helpful to advertising practitioners and other businessmen in making objective decisions about the measurement techniques and services they are using. The effect should be to improve existing methods, and also to help in the development of new ones that are both feasible and that are closely related to the ideal method discussed.

Lack of agreement as to what really is meant by advertising effectiveness presents a problem. To some people, the phrase may mean just the recall of copy points in advertisements, whereas others believe that effectiveness should mean a change in attitudes brought about by the advertising. Still others would prefer to express effectiveness directly, in sales or profit terms.

An "ideal" solution to the conflict among these different points of view is presented by the authors—an operational definition of relative advertising effectiveness. The definition spells out what one would do if there were no restrictions of time, money, techniques, or anything else. The technique involves a new concept that has been dubbed IMP—*I*dealized *M*easurement *P*rocedure.

With this Idealized Measurement Procedure as a basis for comparison, a number of the current syndicated and nonsyndicated measurement techniques are analyzed, and with indications of why each method falls short of the ideal. It is then for the user of advertising to decide whether deviation from the ideal is vital to him for his particular measurement problem.

The authors of this book are to be commended for assembling this analysis on the measurement of advertising effectiveness.

They have "pulled together" some of the principal concepts found in the various books published by the National Industrial Conference Board on advertising measurement. along with the Lucas-Britt book on *Measuring Advertising Effectiveness*, plus additional source materials.

They have also added new insights into advertising theory— especially as to the relationships between measurement results and decision making.

STEUART HENDERSON BRITT
Communications Consultant
Marketing Science Institute

Advertising Measurement and Decision Making

I

Measurement for Advertising Decisions

TECHNIQUES FOR MEASURING ADVERTISING effectiveness are used daily to aid advertisers in making choices among advertising alternatives. Persons seeking reliable measurements of effectiveness often must guess, however, as to which existing techniques are the most appropriate for their needs.

We wish to propose a tool for analyzing and evaluating any technique which purports to measure advertising effectiveness. In order to determine which of the exisiting techniques for measuring effectiveness is most appropriate in a given situation, an understanding is first required of the basic techniques available, their major advantages and disadvantages, and also some insight into the extent to which their results can be relied upon. An idealized measurement procedure has been developed to serve as an *ideal* standard of comparison. Thus, any given technique's deviations from this ideal can be explicitly stated and considered in the light of the relevant costs and benefits.

This standard of comparison or bench mark will help to identify and evaluate the assumptions embodied in any contemporary technique for measuring advertising effectiveness. Consequently, a significant portion of this book is devoted to the development of an idealized measurement procedure, and to providing examples of how it may be used to advantage by both advertising managers and advertising researchers.

For convenience in referring to this standard of comparison in the remainder of this book, the initials *IMP* will be used generally to designate this "Idealized Measurement Procedure." Chapters III, IV, V, and VI especially will focus on this development and provide a framework for systematic analysis of existing measurement techniques.

First, though, in this initial chapter we shall attempt to provide the necessary management and research perspectives. Discussions of measurement frequently begin with the question, "Why measure?" The basic assumption in this book is that the reasons for measuring the effectiveness of advertising are to try to make a specific decision as a result of the measurement, or at least to improve the basis of decision making.

CAN ADVERTISING PERFORMANCE BE MEASURED?

Advertising practitioners, whether associated with advertisers, agencies, or media organizations, are divided among themselves about the feasibility and desirability of trying to measure advertising results. Some advocate measurement because they believe sincerely that it can provide guidance in improving the quality of advertising decisions. Others pay lip service to measurement apparently because it is fashionable to favor a "scientific" approach to business problems. Some frankly and openly shun any effort toward measurement, for reasons varying from "having been burned" to feeling psychologically "threatened" by research procedures.

Attitudes vary widely not only toward advertising measurement, but also about the value of measurement results available from the various measurement services. Here again, some advertising people consider the results invaluable, whereas others believe such services are worthless and perhaps even misleading. Even some who use some of the services are skeptical about their value and yet continue using them for lack of more reliable information sources.

In response to their critics, representatives of measurement services charge that measurement information sometimes is misused. They point out that users must honor the underlying "assumption structure" of any research report. If they ignore them or draw conclusions that exceed the scope of the data, the users are at fault—not they, say the measurement-service people.

The debate over the value of specific measurement services represents only part of the broader question of the feasibility of advertising measurement. From recent marketing literature, one might get one of two different impressions:

1. Concern for measuring the effectiveness of advertisements and advertising campaigns is relatively new.
2. Attempts to improve old measurement procedures and techniques and to develop new ones in the past few years have been eminently successful.

Either of these impressions would be erroneous. While more attention now is being given to improving and developing measurement procedures, certain techniques have been used for decades.

And despite commendable progress in defining and attacking measurement problems, much remains to be done.

Leo Bogart, Executive Vice President and General Manager, Bureau of Advertising of the American Newspaper Publishers Association, has called attention to the "extraordinarily expensive and difficult" problem of relating the results of advertising measurement, usually stated in communication terms, to sales or profit results that are meaningful to the advertiser. As he points out, the businessman's primary interest is to calculate the "effect," or sales return, from his advertising investment.[1]

Furthermore, Blaine Cooke, Marketing Vice President of Trans World Airlines, warns marketing management to accept an obligation to preexamine carefully its commitments of time and money to advertising measurement, considered as separate from other elements in the promotional mix. "The issue is not whether it can be done, but whether it is worth doing."[2]

The problems encountered in understanding and evaluating advertising may appear more formidable than those in engineering, physics, or other "hard" sciences. One explanation for this state of affairs, and a seemingly reasonable one, is that human behavior, the social sciences in general, and advertising in particular lack a well-developed body of theory.

In physics, for example, theory supplies an explanation for the relationships that occur among variables. By contrast, the area of advertising has no generally accepted theory to explain cause-and-effect behavior. A TV advertisement that appears on Monday may in fact be related to a housewife's shopping behavior on Friday. The nature of that relationship is far from clear; cause and effect may be inferred only through a chain of reasoning and not usually by direct measurement.

In the absence of a well-developed body of advertising theory, advertisers must make assumptions about the chain of events that takes place between advertisement exposure and buying behavior. One of the customary assumptions, for example, is that advertisement exposure causes attitude change, and attitude change brings about behavior change. However, some researchers are questioning this sequence of events and are suggesting that behavior change may precede attitude change.[3] Which assumption is correct or whether both are correct under different sets of circumstances is difficult to say without a more complete understanding of the entire advertising process.

A generally accepted body of theory would be a significant step toward greater understanding of how advertising works and how it interacts with the other components of marketing. Correspondingly, our approach to advertising measurement—developing explicit criteria for the evaluation of techniques for measuring advertising effectiveness—is one step toward the formulation of a comprehensive theory of advertising.

WHAT ARE WE MEASURING?

Up to this point the term "advertising" has been used as if it were unambiguous. In practice it means many different things to different people; and the lack of a common definition of the term is undoubtedly partly responsible for differing opinions about measuring its effectiveness.

It should be recognized that advertising is *"any paid form of nonpersonal presentation and promotion of products, services, or ideas by an identifiable individual or organization."* [4]

The purpose of advertising is to change or to reinforce certain aspects of the behavior of people in a direction desired by the sponsor. Further, an advertising campaign is an interrelated set of specific advertisements, along with the media and the schedule of insertions of the advertisements. In other words, an advertising campaign involves three elements:

1. The specific advertisement(s),
2. The specific media vehicles, and
3. The schedule of insertions.

The concept of advertising effectiveness and its measurement is intimately related to the problems of decision making in advertising. In this connection, a decision may be defined as *a conscious choice among alternative courses of action in order to achieve some desired end.*

A source of confusion about advertising measurement has been the fact that decisions involving advertising fall into two classes. There are *marketing decisions* which are made in conjunction with decisions affecting the remainder of the marketing mix, and there are *advertising decisions* which are made somewhat independently.

An example of marketing decisions is the choice of alternative allocations of a promotional budget, where the alternatives are to emphasize media advertising at the expense of perhaps personal selling, or vice versa. One could consider this decision as a choice of spending more or less for media advertising. However, the entire promotional mix is at stake, and not just the advertising budget.

An example of advertising decisions is the choice of specific copy treatment in an advertising campaign. Few if any cases occur where a decision on sales force allocation or a public relations budget would be interdependent with a decision on copy treatment.

Thus, a choice concerning copy normally would be an advertising decision, while the question of budget allocation typically would be a marketing decision. However, some decisions are not as readily classified. In selecting media, an advertising manager might be choosing among two general magazines, such as *Life* and *Look.* Because both magazines are assumed to reach somewhat the same kind of audience, the choice of either one would not be likely to affect decisions outside the advertising area. Here the choice would be an advertising decision.

If, however, the magazines being considered were *Good Housekeeping* versus *Sports Illustrated,* the choice might involve quite different advertising and marketing strategies. For this reason, a media choice in this instance probably would be a marketing decision because of its effect on decisions outside the area of advertising.

To determine how a decision should be classified, it is necessary to examine the particular circumstances of each situation. If the effects of the decision on other decisions outside the advertising area are so slight that they can be disregarded, the decision is an advertising one. At a different time and under different circumstances, a similar question may become a marketing decision. The determining factor is the extent to which the effect of a decision about advertising can be ignored in making other decisions outside the advertising area.

Whether a particular decision is considered "advertising" or "marketing" depends on the information (or assumptions) existing about the interaction of elements in a marketing mix. A decision maker may feel that he can estimate the interactions, and also that the interactions are important enough to consider. In this case he would be likely to consider the broader marketing decision rather than the advertising decision, which is a component of the former.

The reason for making the distinction between the two types of decisions is to help clarify the concept of advertising effectiveness, and highlight some of the problems in measuring effectiveness. The courses of action being considered in a marketing decision are alternative marketing mixes, involving "tradeoffs" among such factors as advertising, personal selling, and sales promotion. When advertising is considered a component in a larger marketing decision, the meaning of the concept "advertising effectiveness" is not clear. Interactions among marketing elements appear to be so complex that one cannot objectively ascribe a specific level of sales to any single factor or group of factors, whether advertising, personal selling, marketing research, or whatnot.

Obviously, however, since executives do make marketing mix decisions, they are able subjectively to estimate the relative potential profitability of alternative mixes without explicitly assigning a figure to each contributory component. This subject was explored by the Marketing Science Institute's book *Promotional Decision Making: Practice and Theory,*[5] and also in another MSI book, *Promotional Decisions Using Mathematical Models.*[6] Two

of the contributors to the latter book, Alfred A. Kuehn, Professor
of Industrial Administration at the Carnegie Institute of Technology, and Albert C. Rohloff, Senior Operations Analyst at Lever
Brothers Co., point out that many advertisers are dissatisfied
with their present approaches to budgeting and allocating advertising funds.

> [These advertisers] intuitively feel, with millions of dollars being spent, that
> significant improvements ought to be possible. . . . It must be recognized
> that sales and market share are functions of many variables in addition to
> advertising. To be sure, aggregate marketing models must inevitably be
> highly simplified descriptions of reality. Nevertheless, is it reasonable to
> assume that an advertising budgeting model which neglects the competitive
> effects of price, product attributes, and retail availability can have much
> utility in highly competitive markets? [7]

Some advertising experiments have attempted to assess the
"contribution" of a specific advertising expenditure to sales.
Even if advertising is omitted from some regions, and run normally in others, and the sales results are compared, some argue
that this is not a legitimate comparison unless a realistic alternative for the advertiser is to exclude advertising from his
marketing mix. In the marketing of most products, such an alternative normally would not be considered. In actual practice, a
marketing strategy without advertising would be quite different
from one in which the advertising was omitted only temporarily.

Throughout the discussion to follow, the term "effectiveness"
will be used. This term is used to denote the degree to which
advertising can change people's external or internal behavior with
respect to an item—product, service, or idea—advertised, and in
the direction desired by the advertiser. This definition is fairly
broad, in the expectation that practically anyone concerned with
such questions should be able to tailor a definition for his own
purposes which, generally speaking, will fall within this scope.
Despite this desired flexibility, our intention in this book is to
give the concept "advertising effectiveness" a more precise meaning than it currently possesses, and furthermore to facilitate
comparisons and selection among alternative measures of effectiveness.

MEASUREMENT AND THE MAJOR ADVERTISING DECISIONS

Since measurements are made in order to improve future decisions, it is useful to identify the major advertising decisions.
The principal advertising decisions involve questions such as:

1. To advertise or not to advertise.
2. How much to spend on advertising.
3. The message and its content.
4. The media and their schedule.

These areas of decision are interdependent, although advertisers and agencies differ in the order in which they approach them.

The first two decisions, concerning whether and how much to advertise, frequently are interrelated with decisions about other parts of a marketing program. A decision about an advertising budget, for example, may be made in connection with decisions about a personal selling budget, a publicity budget, and budgets for other promotional activities. By contrast, the latter two advertising decisions about message content, presentation, and media selection often are made independent of other marketing decisions.

The bulk of measurement efforts have been and still are devoted to the effects of message content and presentation, and media selection. As a result, this report emphasizes these applications of measurement, since the decisions of whether and how much to advertise typically are based more on judgment and experience than on measurement results.

To Advertise or Not to Advertise

The question of whether or not to advertise probably seldom recurs, once a policy to advertise has been adopted. [8] The opportunity for profitable advertising is assumed to exist, and attention tends to be diverted to the specifics of such advertising. This is unfortunate, for a reappraisal of advertising opportunities may on occasion be beneficial.

The information needed to determine advertising's potential profitability is also germane to decisions about budgets, advertisement content, presentation, media, and schedules. Should the decision to advertise be based on actual tests (measurements), these very test results then can be employed to advantage in other directions. Measurements used for budget allocations, conversely, can be helpful in reappraising the advertising opportunities.

To consider fully the implications of the question "Should we advertise?," an executive should be willing to view advertising as interchangeable, at least to some extent, with other forms of promotion. Furthermore, for a completely satisfactory answer to the question, reliable estimates would be required of probable returns from all alternative marketing activities. These might include equivalent outlays for expanding the sales force, building a new distribution center, or improving the product. If approximate returns from such alternatives could be known, an executive might make optimal decisions about his allocation of funds.

With the present state of knowledge, however, it is necessary for the executive to choose an approach, without knowing whether it is the optimal one which can satisfy certain criteria that he has established. [9] Continued research will be able to help reduce the area of uncertainty in deciding whether or not to advertise. This basic question implies the need particularly for well-conceived research experiments aimed at examining alternative promotional inputs and resulting benefits.

Executives of the firms interviewed for the present study devoted less attention to the whether-to-advertise decision than to any other. They seemed to have accepted the value or necessity of advertising as a competitive tactic; they were more concerned with such questions as how much, how, and where to advertise. Since it is difficult to make a conclusive case against advertising, they found it preferable to be "on the safe side" and to continue using advertising.

How Much to Spend on Advertising

The complexity of determining an advertising allowance is implicit in the preceding discussion. Herbert D. Maneloveg, Media Director of Batten, Barton, Durstine & Osborn, Inc., has commented further on the difficulties involved:

> When asked to justify an increase or decrease in advertising budget, we are lost because of an inability to articulate what would happen with the increase or the decrease; if sales go up we credit advertising, if sales go down we blame pricing, distribution, and competition. [10]

The number of dollars spent for advertising by a firm are determined in various ways. To mention a few, the advertising budget may be set through a somewhat arbitrary allocation, historical precedent, budget to fit a specific objective, or any of the four traditional approaches: percentage of sales or profit, unit assessment, competitive parity, and available funds, or various combinations of these. In practice, management frequently may utilize several different methods as the appropriation is set, including applying new approaches such as Operations Research and computer technology. [11]

The Message and Its Content

Research into the message and what it conveys to its audiences has been the subject of varied research studies. Much of this work has centered on concept testing and copy testing of advertisements, using various measures of audience response such as awareness, knowledge, and attitudes. These response measures have covered the complete range from respondents' verbalizations in responding to questions to the subtleties of involuntary eye movements and pupillary dilation as recorded by an eye camera.

These research efforts have been aimed at improving layouts, copy, and formats, as well as providing fresh insights into creative appeals. Depending on what media are employed and on what products or services are being promoted, many important tactical variations are possible for handling message and content.

For individual advertisements, measurements can be made at any of five different "stages" in the advertising development process:

1. Before any move is made in building the physical advertisement or in deciding on its components.
2. As components—headline, captions, illustrations, and so on—are conceived.
3. When the advertisement has been "assembled" in either rough or finished form, but before it is run commercially.
4. When the advertisement is first run commercially but less than full scale.
5. After the advertisement has been run.

Measurements at the first four stages are pretests. Measurement at the fifth stage is a post-test. In a sense, all measurements should be considered pretests in that they are presumably made to influence decisions on later advertisements. By no means are measurements always made at each of the five stages. The fourth stage exists only because a test is being made at that point.

Relatively limited progress has been made, however, in developing rigorous measures suitable for comparing advertising alternatives. While some of the more recent computer-assisted developments in psychometric scaling such as MSI's MAPP (Mathematical Analysis of Perception and Preference) can lead to significant improvements in assessing the effectiveness of the message and its content, it seems likely that essentially subjective evaluations will continue to dominate prevailing practice for some time. Yet these evaluations, when carried out within the IMP framework to be described in this book, can assure higher confidence in the results. The system of assessing new measurement techniques against an idealized standard can provide criteria against which to evaluate both existing and new testing techniques, and to assess measurement progress over time.

The Media and Their Schedules

Most of the information used in media and scheduling decisions is provided by the media, rather than through the research efforts of advertisers and agencies. Syndicated services recently have become an additional information source. While the quantity and variety of available information has increased markedly over the years—moving generally from "circulation" to "audience" data— it is still far from completely satisfactory and is not evenly available from all media or all media vehicles.

The National Industrial Conference Board's report, *Evaluating Media,* describes the factors affecting media decisions and deals with research covering media audiences, exposure to media, and the uses of computers in media selection. [12] The report also proposes several methods for measuring media contributions to advertising effects.

Information for media selection and scheduling, aside from costs, has to take into account the following three considerations:

1. The total audience or potential audience of a specific vehicle in a given medium (reach).
2. The makeup or composition of a vehicle's audience.
3. The contribution of the editorial context to the effects of ads employed with the vehicle on the behavior of its audience (impact).

The first two categories, reach and composition, are properties of the vehicle only. That is, the number and kind of people exposed to the vehicle are independent of the advertising campaign itself. For this reason, techniques for measuring audience size and composition are not discussed in this study. They are considered to be measures of media characteristics, not measures of advertising effectiveness per se.

The overall effectiveness of an advertisement or campaign in a vehicle is believed to depend not only on the vehicle's audience characteristics, but on the editorial environment of the vehicle as well. The impact of the editorial environment may vary from product to product and from advertisement to advertisement, and this is to be taken into account in the discussion below of IMP.

HOW CAN ADVERTISING PERFORMANCE BE MEASURED?

Research approaches for the measurement of advertising performance are either experimental or nonexperimental in design, and they are found in both pre-tests and post-tests of advertising.

Taking the problem area of "how much to spend on advertising" as an example, here are examples of these two approaches:

1. Nonexperimental design, using the analysis of historical data for the purpose of trying to determine how expenditures apparently have affected company sales.
2. Experimentation with various advertising dollar amounts to arrive at what seems to be the most reasonable appropriation in given circumstances.

A good example of a *nonexperimental* study to determine the sales effects of advertising is the research reported by Dr. Kristian S. Palda.[13] He utilized a technique from mathematical statistics—multiple regression analysis—to estimate the long-run effects of advertising expenditures on sales of Lydia Pinkham's Vegetable Compound over the period 1907-1960.

Another *nonexperimental* example of the use of historical data is reported by Kurt H. Schaffir and Earle W. Orr.[14] Using information normally available on a brand's sales, profits, and advertising expenditures, they measured two factors:

> The first factor (a) measures the way in which increased advertising expense leads to diminishing returns in sales. The second factor (b) measures what happens to sales from one year to the next if advertising expenditures are held constant.
>
> These two factors are then applied . . . to estimate the effect on profits of changes in advertising from the present level to a higher or lower one.

In contrast, an example of *experimentation* to estimate sales effects from advertising is offered in the case of Teflon.[15] In a controlled experiment, using television as the prime promotional medium, three levels of expenditure were scheduled in thirteen cities during two test periods—the fall of 1962 and the winter of 1963.

Total Expenditure	Advertising Schedule (one-minute commercials)	
$1,000,000	Fall:	10 commercials
	Winter:	7 "
$500,000	Fall:	5 "
	Winter:	3 "
$250,000	Fall:	5 "
	Winter:	no advertising

Using a crossover experimental design, test and control cities were "switched" part way through the experiment. In each city telephone interviews were conducted with one thousand female heads of households, randomly selected, at the end of each test period. The results indicated that:

1. Sales of Teflon-coated cookware could be increased with a proper level of advertising.
2. Test markets, where advertising on TV was carried on at lower levels, showed no discernible effect on sales.
3. Promotional effort in test markets at the million-dollar level resulted in the doubling of purchases of Teflon-coated cookware as compared with the lower-level of no-advertising test markets.

4. There was strong evidence of a carryover effect of advertising in test cities where promotion was carried on at the million-dollar level of expenditures.

The experiment plus additional research provided convincing evidence that Teflon advertising could work and also indicated the amount of investment needed in the national market to make the advertising profitable.

Results of another controlled experiment to determine the effect of different levels of promotional expenditures on sales of fluid milk were published in 1965.[16] This research was conducted by the United States Department of Agriculture in cooperation with the American Dairy Association. The specific objective of the study was to determine whether increased promotional expenditures by the Association would increase sales of fluid milk enough to justify the added cost.

The annual expenditures for promotion at the time of the test were two cents per capita. The increases in promotional expenditure selected for testing were fifteen and thirty cents per capita on an annual basis. These amounts were large enough to provide a fair test of whether sales could be increased, yet did not exceed an outside figure which the Association reasonably might be expected to sustain under typical operating conditions.

A particular experimental design was used—a Latin square— so that each expenditure level was in effect in each of the six test markets in each six-month period of the test. Consequently, all expenditure levels were tested both in seasons of high consumption and in seasons of low consumption. The statistical technique known as analysis of variance was applied to the experimental data. It revealed that direct effects of different levels of expenditure varied to a significant degree, but that the increased sales of the 15-cent (medium) and 30-cent (heavy) levels of promotion were not equally profitable.

> The medium level increased sales by an average of 13,000 pounds per day per market or 4.5 percent, and heavy promotion increased sales by an average of 17,000 pounds per day per market, or 5.9 percent. These increases include the immediate effect of promotion and the enduring influence which carried over into the six-month period immediately following promotion. The added revenue to dairy farmers from the medium level of promotion was $398,580 . . .
>
> The cost of achieving this increase—the total amount spent for the medium level of promotion—was about $237,530. Thus the net return to farmers was $161,050, a return of 68 percent on their investment. The heavy level of promotion cost $436,313 and produced $521,220 in revenue. The net profit was $84,907, a 19 percent return on the amount invested. Thus, of the two levels of expenditures considered, the medium level was optimal.[17]

Similar controlled experiments have been used to measure other aspects of advertising—particularly in testing the relative effectiveness of two or more alternative campaigns. In all such instances the fundamental plan has been to test an idea or hypothesis and from this to decide an issue which hinges on the outcome of the experiment. This represents the true scientific method, which is conceptually the same no matter what the subject matter, the nature of the scientific inquiry, or the specific technique of measurement.

The controlled-experiment approach and the historical data analysis approach (sometimes referred to as nonplanned experimental) both involve some type of model representing the researcher's beliefs about how advertising expenditures affect sales, market share, or other outcomes of interest. Some researchers, however, are skeptical of what they consider oversimplified models which ignore the effects of other factors that influence sales—factors that may fluctuate at the same time that advertising variations are noted. Clearly, if other things are not equal, then it can be helpful to know the direction and amount of changes of these less obvious variables and the degree to which they may influence the performance being measured.

THE DILEMMA OF ADVERTISING EFFECTIVENESS

In the MSI book, *Promotional Decision Making: Practice and Theory,* extensive observational studies of six consumer goods and six industrial goods companies were reported. Interviews had been conducted with key advertising and marketing executives within each company and with their advertising agency counterparts in both line and staff work. Within these twelve companies, the effectiveness dilemma—the lack of reliable measures of advertising or promotional efficacy—was very apparent.

It was revealed, for example, that only a few studies had been conducted dealing with the effectiveness of the promotional mix, or the particular means of advertising and promotion.

> In one company, most of the research was being devoted to the effectiveness of the advertising message and of individual sales promotion methods . . . In another case the researchers did not, or could not, take advantage of what could be experimented with in the company's market tests that would contribute to the advertising research program . . . In a third company, a member of the marketing research department had produced a simple model for the analysis of the profitability of advertising various categories of existing products. He had produced some intriguing findings, but the advertising manager in this company remained completely unaware of this work. [18]

The study further revealed that although research by advertising agencies into the effectiveness of individual or multiple media was in some cases substantial, their findings and insights were relatively unused by the client firms.

Also, some of the liaison channels to the advertising agencies were observed to be restrictive; and in some cases showed a lack of awareness of, or sensitivity to, opportunities. A mutually planned and reasonably comprehensive research program by the advertising agency and the client corporations was found in only one instance out of twelve.[19]

As to some of the real difficulties involved in attempting to produce reliable measures of advertising effectiveness:

Many of the measurement methods currently employed to estimate the effectiveness of promotion have been inadequately researched regarding their reliability and the value of what they purport to measure. Comprehensive and cooperative research programs are needed since the task exceeds the resources of most individual corporations or professional groups.[20]

Progress in advertising measurement in general, and in advertising effectiveness in particular, is slow and perhaps even disappointingly slow. As Charles Ramond pointed out in an editorial in the first issue of the *Journal of Advertising Research*:

A problem is not attacked, but painfully translated into a set of answerable questions. There are no breakthroughs, only small decreases in the unexplained variance. Instead of final conquest, there will simply be better advertising decisions — measurably better.[21]

At the heart of the problem of measurement of advertising effectiveness is the lack of reliable information about what actually happens between advertisement exposure and some ultimate response. Most people tend to dismiss the problem as being too complex, at least for the time being, and rely on the creative judgment of those whose judgment is believed to be sound.

In an interview, the research director of one advertising agency said:

Measuring advertising effectiveness for products sensitive to advertising can be quite a different story from measuring it for products where advertising has relatively little effect. Furthermore, within a product group, the effect — actual or desired — of advertising for the leader in the field may be quite different from the actual or desired effect of advertising for a lesser brand. To be valid, any measurement procedure would have to recognize these differences.

Implied in this statement is the idea that some syndicated or standardized measurement services might be quite appropriate for one kind of product yet altogether inappropriate for others. For example, the effect of advertising for a particular brand of toothpaste may be quite different from its effect on the promotion of hot-water heaters, where brand identification is either slight or nonexistent.

Furthermore, measuring the effect of advertising for the dominant brand in a product category may require a different approach than for a less popular brand whose market share is considerably smaller. Advertising for the lesser brand could produce a significant gain in market share, while a similar increase for the dominant brand might be extremely difficult or expensive to achieve or measure.

In many cases this dilemma is resolved by using more than one type of measurement for the same advertisement. One of the advertising executives interviewed used as many as seven techniques altogether, varying them according to the type of situation. The idea seems to be that if several different methods produce somewhat similar results, assurance of validity is far greater than if only one method had been used, but that if the different measures do not agree, then decisions about the advertising probably are a matter of judgment.

One agency executive, following an extensive discussion on the shortcomings of existing measurement procedures, qualified his position by calling attention to the shift in measurement emphasis over time. "As recently as ten years ago," he said, "most agency people wanted recall measures to evaluate ads or campaigns. Today most of them want measures of attitude change induced by exposure to the advertising." The question still remains, however, whether attitude change is the correct measure of effectiveness.

Most users who were interviewed seemed to be aware of the limitations of existing techniques. They tend to accept the techniques, however, in somewhat the same spirit that audience ratings are accepted – they may not be good enough, but there is nothing better.

One research director noted that what among theoreticians may be cause for alarm may in practice be a false alarm. Deriding the posture of critics who demand that current practice prove itself to be free of one error or another, he felt instead that critics should prove that current practice leads to wrong decisions before they are taken seriously. He pointed out that most measurement services use samples that have limitations from a theoretical viewpoint, but that even with substantial improvements in their samples, the results are not any different from those previously obtained.

In addition to the sampling problem, other questions are commonly raised in connection with the more widely used pretests and post-tests for measuring the effectiveness of individual advertisements. These questions are quite familiar to advertising researchers. Is questioning of respondents of such a nature as to incline them to assume "expert" roles? Are requisite skills employed to remove the possibility of bias in the questioning of respondents and in interpreting their answers? Can respondents be reasonably expected to give dependable, meaningful answers? Are answers subject to halo effects? Are the conditions of the test too artificial to yield useful answers? Is low cost, simplicity, or speed allowed to outweigh reliability and validity factors? Does achievement of reliability detract attention from validity?

Methodological questions such as these are properly raised in appraising proposed tests and the results of tests. On the subject of recognition measures, Darrell B. Lucas and Steuart Henderson Britt, marketing professors at New York University and Northwestern University, point out that the accuracy of the ratings depends on how much the true facts are diluted and distorted by faults in the basic method or in its execution, and how accurate the scores must be in order to be useful. [22]

If tests seem methodologically satisfactory when judged against such criteria, there remain broader and perhaps more fundamental questions. What is the objective of the test? Of what significance is the objective? Of what significance are different degrees of recognition, recall, and attitude change? What is tested — the advertisement itself or the effect the advertisement has?

It is to these basic issues that this book, with its Idealized Measurement Procedure (IMP) is aimed.

II

Measures of Performance

SINCE ADVERTISING DECISION MAKING usually entails the selection of a course of action from among a set of alternatives, it is helpful to have some measure of advertising effectiveness as a guide to such decisions.

In other words, the basis for the choice among the alternatives can be viewed in terms of some desired effect anticipated from the particular alternative selected. It is at this point that appropriate measurements can be quite helpful in estimating which of the alternative policies may yield the greatest return in terms of impact or effectiveness—and possibly by how much more one alternative is superior to another.

ABSOLUTE VERSUS RELATIVE EFFECTIVENESS

The questions advertisers usually hope to answer by attempts to measure advertising effectiveness are, "How good is the advertising?" or, "What am I 'buying' with my advertising expenditure?" Such questions look for *absolute* measures of advertising quality and of "contribution" to overall sales and profits.

There are many problems in trying to define what one would mean by an absolute measure of advertising quality. Such a measure should enable direct comparison of advertising effectiveness for the same product under different market conditions and for completely different products. For example, if an absolute measure of effectiveness were available, one would say that a television advertising campaign for soap flakes which had a "quality" score of 26 was better than a magazine campaign for an airline with a score of 23. Yet with current knowledge of advertising's effects, such comparisons are meaningless.

It is also difficult to conceive of an absolute measure of advertising's contribution to sales and profit. Except for products for which advertising is marginal activity (that is, it could be eliminated without major marketing changes), to ask what is advertising's "contribution" to total sales of a product is no more relevant than asking for the sales contribution of the accounting department or the company cafeteria—or of the sales force, for that matter.

A much better understanding of marketing than is now available will be required in order to isolate the effects of the advertising elements in a marketing decision. Their "share" to total marketing effectiveness of one marketing alternative versus another generally is obscured by their interaction with other non-advertising elements. The concept of absolute advertising effectiveness, then, is beyond the scope of this report.

Our immediate concern is with a relative measure of advertising effectiveness—to enable an optimal choice from among any number of possible advertising alternatives.

For actual advertising decision making, what is necessary is, first, to specify the alternatives or a feasible set of alternatives within the context of the specific marketing environment, and then to assess the relative advertising effectiveness of one alternative versus another. This assessment may involve a simple estimate of which of the advertising alternatives is best, or a ranking of the alternatives with respect to the decision criterion, or it may be important to indicate the degree of superiority or difference among the different alternatives with respect to the decision criterion.

SOME TYPICAL ADVERTISING EFFECTS

The question of what criteria the advertiser should use in choosing an advertising alternative remains. From among the many possible effects of advertising, one or more must be selected to designate specifically what the advertiser wants to accomplish with his advertising. It is these selected effects that the advertising decision maker would like to use as his criteria for choosing among alternatives to which the term "effectiveness" shall apply.

Many of the possible advertising effects, such as brand awareness, usually are not of interest in themselves. They are of interest only insofar as they contribute to the achievement of corporate goals, such as greater profits or higher corporate prestige.

When a business firm employs advertising as a promotional and selling tool, its advertising may have a variety of effects on the response (behavior) patterns of household consumers, business users, dealers, distributors, competitors and others. Following are a few examples of the possible advertising effects:

Consumer Effects of Advertising

Advertising obviously can and does have many effects on consumers, including:

I. *Verbal Responses on*

    1. The ways in which people answer questions about the ad, saying whether they:
       a. recall seeing or hearing the advertisement;
       b. liked or were influenced by the advertisement.
    2. The ways in which people answer questions about the product, saying whether they:
       a. are familiar with the product;
       b. express favorable opinions about the product;
       c. express an intention to buy the product;
       d. have bought the product.

II. *Nonverbal Responses on*

    1. The ways in which people actually behave (nonverbally) toward the product:
       a. the choices they make in a laboratory situation;
       b. whether or not they shopped for the product and inquired about it;
       c. whether or not they purchased the product;
       d. how much of the product they purchased;
       e. the ways in which they use the product.
    2. The physiological and physical responses of the people.

The above list is not intended to be complete. It is meant only to indicate the range of ways in which advertising might affect consumers.

Trade Effects of Advertising

A consumer advertising campaign, by its impact on members of the trade, could affect:

    1. The readiness with which the company's representatives are received and the ease of their selling job;
    2. The purchase of the product by the trade;
    3. The frequency and magnitude with which the trade promotes the product;
    4. The attitudes of people in the trade;
    5. The price which the trade is willing to pay for the product.

This is a partial list only of the possible trade effects of consumer advertising.

Other Effects of Advertising

The use of an advertising campaign may affect the nature of *competitive actions.* For example, budget increases may be matched or exceeded by competitors. A particularly strong theme, or the use of an unusual medium, may cause a direct response by the competition.

Employees of the company may be affected by its advertising. A campaign emphasizing product quality may cause production workers to be more careful about quality. Similarly, a campaign stressing new uses for a product may motivate salesmen to focus their presentations toward new ways to use the product.

In addition, other people in society, government, financial institutions, and so on may be affected either positively or negatively by an advertising campaign. As a result, their anticipated and actual reactions may affect various aspects of the company's activities.

HIERARCHY OF EFFECTS

Since most advertising is sponsored by profit-seeking organizations, the goals of these organizations include the achievement, maintenance, or growth of short-run or long-run net profits or return on funds employed. Certain factors may be of interest, however, beyond their ultimate effect on profits. A company's executives may be interested in social as well as financial goals, for example; thus, if a particular advertising program were to affect either the employees' welfare or the country's political system, the executives would consider these factors as well as net profits.

Nevertheless, earnings are a measure of results which seems to be more generally accepted than any other, and they obviously are important to the organization's existence. Since advertising is an integral part of a company's total operations, the ultimate ends of advertising should coincide with the company's fundamental aims.

Therefore, the concept of advertising effectiveness will be identified with the criterion on which one would ideally like to base advertising decisions—namely, relative contribution to profits. This means, then, that the meaning of "relative advertising effectiveness" should be *the discounted present value of the difference in long-term profits which would be produced via the choice of one advertising alternative over another.*

Ideally, if the decision maker were to know this precise value for each of the advertising alternatives, it is assured that this would be sufficient information on which to base the vast majority of his advertising decisions. Although such knowledge is realistically impossible, it still pays to state the ideal and to examine the operational problems of using it in practice.

The use of difference in profits as the criterion for relative advertising effectiveness not only is theoretically sound but is the most desirable one from a management point of view. To a large extent, however, it is not directly usable as a measure because advertising is only a partial determinant of sales. As a result, advertisers often use other effects as substitute measures of advertising effectiveness. In so doing, they imply a willingness to accept a causal or at least predictive relationship between changes in a person's knowledge or attitude about a product or service and changes in his purchases with respect to that product or service. This idea is embodied in the theory of a "hierarchy of effects." One example is:

1. Unawareness
2. Awareness
3. Knowledge
4. Liking
5. Preference
6. Conviction
7. Purchase

The hierarchy-of-effects theory is a hypothesized description of an individual going through a number of steps of increasing commitment to action, perhaps skipping one or more steps on his way through.

The rationale for using one of the intermediate steps to *pretest* the performance of advertising is that if advertisement A brings more people than advertisement B to a particular step in the hierarchy, then the use of advertisement A should ultimately result in more sales than the use of advertisement B.

The rationale for the use of the hierarchy approach in post-testing of advertising is similar. Its use in post-measurement is best exemplified by the proposals of Russell Colley in his DAGMAR book ("Defining Advertising Goals for Measuring Advertising Results"), namely, the setting of a goal on an intermediate stage of the hierarchy and the measurement of the extent to which that goal is achieved.

However, a considerable body of evidence is being accumulated to the effect that the hierarchy-of-effects theory may not be an adequate representation of the process of progressive commitment leading to an individual's purchase behavior. This point will be discussed further in Chapter III.

Without the hierarchy-of-effects theory, most of the current rationale for measuring the effectiveness of advertising in terms of communications effects would disappear. Hence, this report proposes an alternative theory on which to base the use of communications measures for the purpose of making equal cost advertising decisions.

Advertising decisions may be differentiated into those involving

alternatives of roughly equal costs and those with alternatives that vary appreciably in cost. For both types of decisions, the decision maker's objective is to choose the alternative with the highest relative effectiveness—that is, the greatest present value of contribution to profits. Yet the distinction is important in that the information requirements for the two categories differ markedly.

The majority of advertising decisions are equal cost decisions. This group includes most decisions concerning copy, creative treatments, media mixes within fixed budgets, timing of advertising and many others. Most advertising decisions involving appreciable cost differences among the alternatives usually turn out upon close examination to be marketing decisions rather than purely advertising decisions. That is, the large variations among the alternatives in expenditures for advertising may have an appreciable effect on the budgeting for other marketing activities.

There are cases, however, in which strictly advertising alternatives have appreciably different costs. As an example, if the choice were between setting a media budget at $2 million or $2.25 million, and the difference was not to be allocated to any other activity except advertising, that would represent an unequal cost advertising decision.

In equal-cost advertising decisions, the alternative which produces the greatest sales also ensures the greatest contribution to profits. For this class of decisions, then, the estimated value of relative revenues may be used as the criterion of effectiveness. In making equal-cost decisions, there is no need to determine *how much* better one alternative is than another. To make a perfect decision, it is necessary only to rank the alternatives in terms of expected revenue and to choose the one ranked first.

Measurement for decision making with unequal cost advertising alternatives becomes more complex. If it happens that a less expensive alternative scores higher than a more expensive alternative on a factor that is highly correlated with relative sales effectiveness, the cheaper alternative is a fairly easy choice. However, if the more expensive alternative scores higher, this is not enough information to warrant its selection.

To know which of the alternatives will produce the greatest present relative revenues is not sufficient; since the costs differ, one must know *how much* the differences in revenues are likely to be. Given that information, one can use marginal analysis to estimate the relative contribution to profits of the alternatives, and then compare the contributions to profits with the relative costs to determine whether the higher cost alternatives justify the extra expenditures. Clearly, simple ranking in this case would be inadequate.

The crucial difference between equal- and unequal-cost advertising decisions is that for the former it is necessary only to know which of the alternatives is best with respect to revenues produced, while for the latter one must estimate the magnitude of the difference in revenues and costs to make a decision. Unequal-cost decisions, therefore, require a much higher level of information. In this book we are concerned primarily with equal-cost decisions.

CORRELATES OF EFFECTS

To make equal-cost advertising decisions preferable to mere coin flipping, a process is required that can select alternatives better than average. If the process used involves some sort of measurement, a positive relationship is needed between what is measured and the true effectiveness of the alternative.

Suppose, for example, that the decision involves a choice among alternative creative treatments for a television campaign. One campaign—although it is not known which—is really most effective; that is, will produce most revenues and profits. One of the alternatives is really second best, etc.

Suppose, further, that a score is assigned to each alternative by testing one representative commercial from each campaign via a theater pretest. One of the commercials will achieve the highest score, another second highest, etc.

If the commercial which scores highest is more likely to be associated with a campaign with a high rank in true effectiveness than one that scores lower, the pretest has at least some validity. An expression of the relationship between two measures, in this case the true effectiveness and the pretest score, is their correlation coefficient. An expression of the relationship between two sets of ranks is their rank correlation coefficient.

There are primarily two reasons for the use of a measure of rank correlation. First, most tactical advertising decisions require only rank information. That is, a choice among alternatives can be based on reliable information about which alternative ranks first.

Second, rank correlations between a test measure and the standard are likely to be much more stable than standard statistical correlation. The statistic produced by the standard will be incremental sales of one alternative versus another at specific points in time and place. The amount of the incremental sales produced is likely to be strongly affected by competitive and economic conditions, whereas test scores are likely to be much less affected by these. Hence, there easily could be instability over time in the statistical correlations between scores on a particular measurement technique and the incremental sales derived from the standard. The rankings, however, are much less likely to be affected in this manner.

Unfortunately, when the alternatives to be evaluated represent appreciably different costs, as in a choice among different budgets, ranking based on sales does not provide sufficient information

with which to make a choice. To be useful, a measure of advertising effectiveness for such decisions must bear a strong functional
relationship to the incremental sales as measured by the standard.
With the exception of a market test, available services and techniques do not seem appropriate for evaluating budget decisions;
it is unlikely they would show a sufficiently strong relationship to
incremental sales. Hence, the following discussion of the various
assumptions is limited to the case of equal cost advertising alternatives, for which the rank requirement is sufficient.

For two measures to be positively correlated, there need be
no causal link between them. They must only be related in such a
way that an advertising alternative that scores well on one measure
tends to score well on the other, although they may differ in any
particular case.

For example, it is not unusual that an advertising campaign
that will tend to cause more people to purchase a product than
would alternative campaigns also will tend to cause people to
answer attitudinal questions more favorably in a pretest. This
relationship, if proven valid for a number of alternatives, can be
expressed as a positive correlation between the pretest scores and
the true relative effectiveness of the alternatives. But for such a
relationship it should not be assumed that those whose attitudes are
favorably affected by the advertising will necessarily be among
those whose purchases are favorably affected.

Since the attitudinal measure associated with the alternatives
is correlated with their true relative effectiveness, the alternative
which would cause the greatest shift in attitude probably would be
among the best in actual effectiveness as well. Hence, in view of
this correlation, the attitudinal measure may be used as a substitute for true effectiveness for the purpose of deciding among these
equal-cost alternatives.

To provide a basis for the use of communications measures as
substitutes for measures of actual effectiveness in equal-cost
advertising decisions, one need only assume a reasonably high
correlation between the communication measure and what would
result if actual effectiveness were measured. This basis for the
use of communications measures might be termed the assumption
of *correlates-of-effects.*

This correlates-of-effects assumption requires less stringent
assumptions about the relationship between communications measures and relative revenues than does the hierarchy-of-effects
theory for equal-cost decisions. Yet the correlates-of-effects
assumption offers no insight, as does the hierarchy-of-effects
theory, into the ways in which advertising influences purchase
decisions. Therefore, the hierarchy-of-effects theory, if ultimately
proved valid, would be preferred. If it cannot be proved valid, then
the assumption of correlates-of-effects may be useful.

There is also the possiblity that both will be proved inadequate.
This would mean that very little relationship exists between

measures of advertising communication and measures of true relative effectiveness. In this case, no justification exists for the use of communication measures as substitutes for true relative effectiveness.

These comments, of course, apply only to equal-cost advertising decisions. With unequal-cost advertising decisions, much more information is needed. In order to use substitute measures of advertising performance for deciding among unequal cost alternatives, one must be able to translate a unit difference in the substitute measure into the corresponding difference in the true measure of effectiveness—present value of relative contribution to profits. Since this value is very likely to be different for different products and even for the same product at different times, such translation represents a formidable obstacle.

SOME IMPLICATIONS

This chapter has provided a theoretical foundation for an approach to measuring advertising effectiveness for the purpose of making advertising decisions.

First, a distinction between advertising and marketing decisions was made. The measurement of advertising effectiveness was considered only with respect to advertising decisions.

Second, a distinction was made between relative and absolute effectiveness. This report treats only relative effectiveness, which is sufficient for advertising decision making purposes.

Third, a criterion of effectiveness was suggested. It is the present value of the difference in long-term profits which would be produced via the choice of one advertising alternative over another.

Fourth, the theory of a hierarchy-of-effects as a rationale for the use of communications effects as measures of advertising performance was discussed.

Fifth, a distinction was made between equal- and unequal-cost advertising decisions. The former requires a much lower level of information than the latter.

Finally, the assumption of correlates-of-effects was proposed as a substitute for the hierarchy-of-effects theory, should the latter prove inadequate. The proposed assumption would serve as a basis for the use of communications measures of advertising performance, as substitutes for sales or profit measures of performance in equal-cost advertising decisions.

III

Comparison of Idealized
Measurement Procedure With
Other Techniques

IN ORDER TO EXAMINE in detail the assumptions associated with the use of particular advertising measurement techniques, it will be helpful to have a framework for analyzing these techniques according to attributes common to them all. Virtually every technique for measuring advertising effectiveness attempts to answer the following questions:

1. What is the scope of advertising being measured?
2. What audience response are we looking for?
3. How realistic are the conditions of test exposure?
4. Are the measurements being made sufficiently precise, yet tolerable?
5. Is the sample representative of the audience?
6. How are alternatives compared, and is there a standard?
7. What do the data handling procedures involve?

With this framework for analysis, it will be possible to specify a theoretical ideal standard for each attribute. That is, if money, time and other considerations were no object, and if practicality could be ignored, the ideal approach would be how one would handle each attribute.

It is as though one could call upon a genie for a perfect procedure, and all that had to be done was to specify one's idealized desires concerning each of the foregoing seven attributes. Clearly, one could not do better by any merely mortal means!

Taken together, the seven attributes above may be thought of as an *ideal* measure of advertising effectiveness. In fact, what would emerge if this ideal could be implemented would be what advertising people *should* mean when they use the term "advertising effectiveness."

This collection of *ideal* attributes (unattainable) will be referred to by the acronym, *IMP—Idealized Measurement Procedure.*

Actual measurement techniques differ from each other and from IMP in one or more ways. By identifying the attributes of actual measurement techniques, one can readily make a point-by-point comparison of each technique.

An examination of the differences between a given technique and IMP will show where compromise assumptions are needed to accept the technique for measuring advertising effectiveness. Some of these assumptions may be readily acceptable; others may be questionable; still others may be totally unacceptable. In any case, by making these assumptions explicit, the techniques can more readily be evaluated by using both research results and management judgment to decide the extent to which a technique's assumptions ought to be accepted.

In the present chapter (see p. 37ff) is a chart of COMPARISONS OF *IDEALIZED MEASUREMENT PROCEDURE* (IMP) WITH VARIOUS ADVERTISING MEASUREMENT TECHNIQUES. It illustrates the types of analysis that can be made, based on a comparison with the Idealized Measurement Procedure.

SYNDICATED TECHNIQUES

Of the eleven examples of measurement services shown on the chart, the seven *syndicated* services are:

Audience Studies, Inc.
Gallup & Robinson Magazine Impact Survey
  (Aided Recall)
Gallup & Robinson Total Prime Time (TPT)
Marder Ad Evaluation Program
Milwaukee Advertising Laboratory
Schwerin Standard TV Testing Service
Starch Readership Service

A brief description of these syndicated measurement services follows:

1. Audience Studies, Inc.

The following is adapted from information supplied by Audience Studies, Inc. in July, 1967: Audience Studies, Inc. (ASI) operates a theater for testing television commercials and programs. Subjects to be exposed are selected by a quota sample based on age, sex, socio-economic status, and television viewing habits. Interviewers go to high traffic centers in the Los Angeles metropolitan area (such as shopping centers) and screen a group of people to produce a standard sample of 250.

Subjects selected are invited to the test theater. To begin the test, participants fill out a brief questionnaire on demographic and viewing data. At this time, they also indicate their initial preferences for products to be awarded as door prizes at the end of the session.

After completing these questionnaires, subjects see a control cartoon, followed by either a new television show or a new installment of an existing television show. The show is presented without commercials and is followed by a program questionnaire.

Three to five television commercials are then shown, one of which is a control commercial. These represent three to five different products. Following each commercial, subjects are asked to complete a questionnaire indicating their opinions about the commercials and products. Additional comments of a small independent subsample also are tape recorded.

In the final test segment another television show is presented and questionnaires completed. After seeing another control cartoon, subjects are asked again for their product preferences in connection with the awarding of door prizes. During both television shows and commercials, one-half of the audience consciously operates individual recorder dials, while the other half responds subconsciously through finger sensors. These provide a record of reactions during shows and commercials, in addition to the written questionnaires completed at the end of the show or commercial.

The factor measured is change in product preference between pre-exposed and post-exposed choices. The assumption is that exposure to the commercials brought about the preference change. To minimize the possible influence of the master of ceremonies on subjects, ASI prescribes the timing, format, and even the pronunciation of individuals who supervise the showings.

2. Gallup & Robinson, Inc. Magazine Impact Surveys (Aided Recall)

The following is adapted from Darrell Blaine Lucas and Steuart Henderson Britt, *Measuring Advertising Effectiveness* (New York: McGraw-Hill Book Co., 1963), pp. 74-76; and from information supplied by Gallup & Robinson, Inc. in July, 1967.

A Gallup & Robinson interviewer begins the aided-recall interview by showing the cover of the measured issue. Before the respondent can qualify for the advertising questioning, he must demonstrate that he is an issue reader by describing at least one article or picture story. The table of contents may be used for prompting.

Readers who are thus qualified are next shown groups of brand/corporate names including all half-page or larger advertisers in the issue. They are told that some names in each group were not advertised in the issue.

Respondents are asked to state which advertisements they think they recall seeing. The interviewer next asks a series of open-end questions about each product or advertiser mentioned, to prove ad recall and determine idea communication and buying attitude. Responses from 200 men and 200 women for each issue of a general magazine are recorded verbatim.

Three measures are produced from these responses:

1. Proved Name Registration (PNR) is based on the percent of readers of the issue who document ad recall by describing specific elements of the advertisement. The number then is adjusted for a number of factors, including cost of the advertisement and the characteristics of the issue under study. The resultant index number permits comparative analysis.
2. Idea Registration shows the extent to which those who can describe the ad "play back" each copy point.
3. Favorable Buying Attitude is the extent to which those who describe the ad also attribute to the ad favorable attitudes toward the product, product ideas, or company.

Product-group norms for each of the three measurements exist to permit evaluations of ad performance. Thus, an advertiser can diagnose the strengths and weaknesses of his own pattern of performance. For example, he may achieve high Proved Name Registration but low Idea Registration. Conversely, he might produce high idea communication but over a smaller audience than desired as indicated by a low PNR score.

These techniques are applied both in pretest and post-test situations.

3. Gallup & Robinson, Inc. – Total Prime Time (TPT)

The following is adapted from Daniel M. Lissance, "Some Important Things I Believe A Young Account Representative Should Know About Creative Research," a publication of the same name by the Committee on Client Service, American Association of Advertising Agencies, June, 1965; and from information supplied by Gallup & Robinson, Inc. in July, 1967.

The surveys are a series of aided, delayed-recall telephone studies conducted at frequent intervals during the year. For each survey a modified probability sample of 2,800 Philadelphia men and women, 18 years and older, are interviewed regarding their previous evening's television viewing during prime time hours. Households comprising the sample are selected at random from residential listings in telephone directories from metropolitan and suburban Philadelphia. Approximately 85 percent of all households in the Philadelphia area have telephone service.

With the aid of a program roster, viewers are asked to plot their viewing pattern during the previous evening for all half-hour time segments in which they were actively watching all or nearly all the time. Following this, respondents are read a list of 15 brand names for products or services advertised within each respondent's viewing pattern (including station breaks). The respondent is asked to indicate whether or not he recalls seeing each product or service advertised "last night." For each commercial recalled, the respondent is asked a series of open-end questions designed to determine recall of specific copy points, attitudinal reactions, and persuasiveness.

From the data obtained, four measures are produced:

1. Commercial Recognition (CR) reflects an initial level of perception based on the percent of viewers exposed to the commercial who "claim" recall of the product or service advertised.
2. Proved Commercial Registration (PCR) is a relatively more intense level of perception, based on the percent of exposed viewers who "prove" recall by accurately describing the commercial concerned.
3. Idea Registration shows the extent to which those "proving" recall of the commercial can play back individual copy points.
4. Favorable Buying Attitude is the extent to which those "proving" recall of the commercial also attribute to the commercial favorable attitudes toward the product, product ideas, or company.

Product-group norms for each of the four measurements exist to permit evaluation of commercial performance against the communication objectives desired by the advertiser. Subscribers to the service receive scores for both their own commercials and those of competitors.

4. Marder Ad Evaluation Program

The following is adapted from information supplied by Eric Marder Associates, Inc. in July, 1967.

The method of testing is that of a controlled experiment. The experiment is conducted among *Saturday Evening Post* subscribers. The total sample for each study consists of 4,800 telephone interviews with respondents in *Post* subscriber households (2,400 men and 2,400 women respondents). Interviews are carried out in

New York, Chicago, and Philadelphia. Each of the samples of 2,400 men and 2,400 women is divided into three randomly equivalent subgroups of 800 respondents each. Subgroup A receives ad A, subgroup B receives ad B, while subgroup C receives no ad and is used as a control group. The ads are inserted in copies of the *Post* in the course of production, and the modified issues are not identifiable as such.

Beginning two days after receipt of the issue and continuing for a four-day period, respondents are contacted and interviewed over the telephone. An identical interview is used for all respondents, and test ads are not mentioned. The interviewer simply identifies herself, and proceeds at once to ascertain awareness and attitude for a variety of products. The respondent has no reason to connect the interview, which is similar to an ordinary general-purpose consumer survey, with the *Post.*

Any differences in awareness and attitude (beyond sampling variations) either among the test groups or between the test groups and the control group are attributed to the test ads. Thus, ad rankings depend on the degree to which ads succeed in changing how respondents think and feel about advertised products, and do not rely on what respondents think of the ads themselves.

5. Milwaukee Advertising Laboratory

The following is adapted from a report published by the Advertising Research Foundation, *Commentary #1, Milwaukee Advertising Laboratory,* 1965; and from information supplied by the Milwaukee Advertising Laboratory in July, 1967.

The Milwaukee Advertising Laboratory is a project designed to provide a set of controlled conditions in a natural setting within which effectiveness of newspaper, newspaper supplement, and television advertising can be measured. By making special arrangements, direct mail and magazine advertising also can be tested. Using the Laboratory, an advertiser can give differential advertising treatment to two matched Milwaukee markets. Each subscriber has sole use of the Laboratory facilities for his product class during the period he participates, which may be from six months to three years. This means that competitive activity cannot affect the two markets differently.

The four counties in the Greater Milwaukee area are divided into two matched markets, Market A and Market B. These markets are matched in terms of demographics as well as in past purchase activity. Within each of the two markets consumer panels have been selected in order to record purchases in weekly diaries. A standard size panel in each market consists of 750 families. However, a third panel of 750 families is available; half of the members of this panel are in Market A and half in Market

B. This third panel permits an advertiser to test more media combinations than would be possible with the two standard panels.

The participating media in the Laboratory are the *Milwaukee Journal, This Week* magazine, the *Journal's* own Sunday supplement, and three of the four Milwaukee television stations. Split-runs of the *Journal* and its supplement are distributed in such a way that residents of each market receive only one of the two test ads. In addition, each of the sample families has a muter attached to its television set (or sets) to control commercial exposure on the set. The muter may be activated by an electronic signal incorporated in a television tape or may be manually controlled at the transmitter. The muter permits instantaneous cut-off and recovery of sight and sound in such a way that there is no interference with preceding or subsequent broadcasting sequences.

Advertisers using the Laboratory can obtain continuing measures of product movement in households exposed to the varying combinations of print and broadcast conditions. Each advertiser receives volume and brand purchase data for his particular product group.

6. Schwerin Standard TV Testing Service

The following is adapted from Robert D. Buzzell, "Predicting Short-Term Changes in Market Share as a Function of Advertising Strategy," *Journal of Marketing Research,* I (August, 1964), pp. 27-31; and from information supplied by Schwerin Research Corporation in July, 1967.

The Schwerin Research Corporation offers basically three television testing services. The most familiar of the three is the Standard Testing Service, and details of this service are summarized below. In addition, Schwerin offers an optional Extended Service, which permits detailed probing into respondents' feelings, attitudes, and comprehension. This service may be incorporated into test designs if greater diagnostic information is desired. The third television service is a Channel Choice test, wherein the members of the audience have the option of watching either of two television programs shown simultaneously on two screens.

In the Standard Testing Service, as well as in the other television testing services, a sample is drawn by selecting names at random from residential telephone directories in metropolitan areas. Tests are conducted mainly in New York City and Chicago, with a small percentage of the testing carried on in other United States cities. Schwerin also has testing facilities in two Canadian cities—Toronto and Montreal.

Those whose names are drawn are invited to attend a theater preview of a television program. An average audience size is 300 people in New York, and 600 to 700 in Chicago, even though the non-response rate among those invited sometimes is as high as 75 percent.

Prior to seeing the television program, each respondent is asked to state a brand preference in each of three product categories. The respondent is told that a drawing will be held later, and that the brand selected is the one he will receive if his name is drawn.

The audience then sees a television program that includes test commercials for one brand in each of the three product categories. After seeing the program each respondent is asked again to indicate his brand preference in each product group.

This testing procedure supplies two basic statistics:

1. The percentage of respondents expressing a preference for a brand *before* exposure to a test commercial, and
2. The percentage expressing preference *after* exposure.

The net change is one measure of the effect of the commercial message. A subsidiary statistic is the *average* change in preference associated with exposures to commercials in a given product class. Schwerin Research Corporation compiles averages or norms for each product class on an annual basis.

7. Starch Readership Service

The following is adapted from Darrell Blaine Lucas and Steuart Henderson Britt, *Measuring Advertising Effectiveness* (New York: McGraw-Hill Book Co., 1963), p. 51; and from information supplied by Daniel Starch and Staff in July, 1967.

Interviews are carried out with 100 to 150 men and 100 to 150 women on each issue studied of magazines of general interest. This sample of 200 to 300 sets of responses is collected from some 15 to 30 different areas in the United States. For magazines of primary interest to only one sex, 150 interviews may be carried out with readers of that sex.

To qualify for an interview, respondents must state that prior to the interview they read the issue of the magazine under study. As the interviewer goes through the magazine with the respondent, the respondent states whether and to what extent he or she read each advertisement a half-page or larger in that issue. The scores reported are:

Noted. The percent of readers of the magazine who report they had previously seen the advertisement in the particular magazine.

Seen-associated. The percent of readers who report they have seen or read any part of the advertisement that clearly indicates the name of the product (or service) or advertiser.

Read most. The percent of readers who not only looked at the advertisement, but who report that they *read more than half* of the total written material in the ad.

The Starch organization also can supply annual *Adnorms* data for comparison purposes. These are the average scores for the previous two years for all advertisements tested by Starch. The *Adnorms* are given separately for each product class, by size of space and color of ads. Within each product class, separate *Adnorms* are provided for men and women for each magazine.

NONSYNDICATED TECHNIQUES

The *nonsyndicated measurement* techniques included as examples are:

1. market test
2. on-air TV test
3. psychogalvanometer test
4. split-run test

A brief description of each of these techniques and services follows, as condensed from Darrell Lucas and Steuart Henderson Britt, *Measuring Advertising Effectiveness* (New York: McGraw-Hill Book Co., 1963).

1.   Market Test

. . . Using controlled advertising situations in which intensity and type of promotion varied, the results of one study suggested that by use of a mathematical model the quantities needed to evaluate and compare alternative promotional campaigns could be computed. But there are reservations and limitations . . .

Essentially there are two ways of obtaining marketing data for mathematical evaluations of advertising expenditures . . . [There are attempts to analyze relationships under normal conditions as well as controlled experiments using some type of experimental design.] While this [first] approach is centered upon wholly normal advertising conditions, it is beset with the many variables in promotional efforts and marketing conditions . . . Usually there is no such thing as holding other promotional activities *constant,* since they are not normally constant. . . .

The alternative to retrospective study of company marketing records is to permit some control of promotional efforts for the purpose of making advertising research more definite. Control may take such forms as holding other promotional efforts fairly constant while varying the application of advertising—or setting aside selected marketing areas or segments for experimental advertising study . . .

The ideal research, based on correlation of variables, calls for complete experimental design in which all variables are accounted for or actually controlled. Such experiments, usually local, make it possible to study the effects of varied advertising and to compare different advertising copy and strategies in selected markets. Some of the problems include variations in the operations of competitors, basic variations in test markets, changes related to time, and completely controlled promotion. Decisions must be objectively scheduled—never to play a hunch or to exploit an opportunity, as in normal business. The experimental approach is certainly the best way to obtain data on advertising influence, but the ideal advertising experiment has not yet been worked out.

2. On-Air TV Test

A description of a Batten, Barton, Durstine, and Osborn on-air testing technique is included because it contains most of the elements of any on-air testing procedure.

The program, a first-run adventure series, provides the agency with three minutes of commercial time to be used in any combination of time units. The program rating in a city with only a single television station runs from 20 to 25. Interviewing is done by telephone with samples of 1,000 which, as indicated by the rating, obtain 200 to 250 viewers.
Some of the special features of the method are:

1. All commercials are tested as they will be viewed on the air under in-home conditions.
2. Each person is individually interviewed within two hours of seeing the show.
3. A relationship between the commercial and the program is established.
4. Because of the availability of three commercial minutes each week, the cost can be carried across two or more commercials.

The viewing conditions are natural and, in contrast with tests using theater projection before groups, the sample tends to be more typical of the program audience. The sample for the tests is systematically selected from the local telephone directory, and only one viewer is interviewed in any one home.
The first question in the interview may be, "If you were to go shopping right now, what brand of (product) would you buy?" This is asked in regard to each of the product categories being studied that night. An inquiry about television viewing that night follows; and if the respondent indicates he had watched the show, he is asked to relate the events of the show in order that his exposure may be verified. Verified viewers then become the basis for measuring the commercial.

Testing of commercial awareness begins with the unaided-recall question, "What products do you remember having seen advertised?" Aid is then given in the form of mention of specific product categories under test, followed by measures of specifically recalled points of the commercial.

Additional questions may also be asked regarding the believability, importance, or uniqueness of ideas featured in the commercial.

The significance of the introductory question regarding brand preference of products lies in the comparison between those later found to be exposed or unexposed to the commercial.

3. Psychogalvanometer Test

There are many techniques which utilize laboratory testing equipment in order to measure physical responses to various stimuli. The psychogalvanometer is used to illustrate how these laboratory techniques may be compared with other techniques. Lucas and Britt describe this technique as follows:

> The *psychogalvanometer,* which keeps a record of changes in galvanic responses, has also been developed into a group-testing instrument. Each participant has one hand or finger attached to an electrode, but is free to observe and react to advertisements. Excitement is known to increase sweating and thus reduce electrical resistance on the slick surface; it is also possible that nerve activity, which is basically electrical, contributes to the measured changes recorded by the instrument.

> In any case, reactions indicated by a psychogalvanometer are amazingly fast, considering that they represent somatic effects of ideas. Within two or three seconds an initial response to a test advertisement is indicated, and this may be followed by ten to twenty seconds of more steady reaction . . . The psychogalvanometer is a completely objective measuring instrument. The question of validity, for advertising research, is another matter. Certainly interpretations of the measuring of galvanic patterns have not become definitive. Extreme fluctuations of the record may indicate excitement, attraction, repulsion, perplexity, or what? Each test subject has a different basic level at the start of every test and, considering the atypical conditions of advertising exposure, it is difficult to know how the galvanic record relates to normal advertising response. It can be said with assurance, of course, that advertisements producing little galvanic change are probably too neutral to cause much reaction or response under normal circumstances.

It should be noted that most laboratory techniques which attempt to relate physiological responses to advertising effectiveness have basically the same assumption structure.

4. Split-Run test

> Much of the confusion in evaluating inquiries from advertisements—with or without coupons—can be resolved through the use of split runs in the same

issue of the same publication. Many publications permit an advertiser to use the same space for two or more copy variations in systematic rotation throughout the entire circulation. If it is desired to test two advertisements, every other copy coming off the press will carry the same insertion. This permits simultaneous circulation of two or more advertisements in identical editorial surroundings with comparable audiences.

If inquiries or mail orders are the only objective of two advertisements and if there is a statistically important difference in returns, the interpretation of a split-run is simple. If, however, the aim is to test different copy elements or to estimate impact on the whole audience, many more precautions are needed. Variations of basic appeal, displayed in dissimilar layouts with varying emphasis upon the offer or coupon, become too complicated for ready analysis. If there are also variations in the nature of wording of the offer or structure of the coupon, little analysis is possible.

On the other hand, responses to offers buried in the running test where only one copy element has been changed may provide convincing evidence of direct action and possibly of general reader interest. Conclusions should never be drawn before a thorough appraisal of all internal and external factors has been made.

These techniques and services have been selected because they are frequently used, are familiar to many advertising people, or contain some unusual or interesting attributes. Clearly, there are other services available; this listing is not meant to be exhaustive or even completely representative. Furthermore, most of these syndicated services offer other types of advertising and marketing measurement information in addition to the particular service shown. No endorsement or criticism of any technique or service is intended either by its inclusion or omission.

The characteristics shown for each service or technique represent their status as of July, 1967, at which time several of the services were revising or expanding their range of tests. As a result, a few details may be out of date.

Both the accompanying fold-out Chart and the text of this chapter supplement each other and are intended to be examined together. Each attribute of the idealized method is specified in detail in this chapter and also outlined in the Chart. Corresponding attributes of the actual measurement techniques used as examples also are noted so that they may be readily compared with IMP; and the various terms used in the Chart are explained.

Since IMP is an ideal, it is not a procedure that can be completely implemented. The seven ideal attributes are intended only as standards against which actual techniques can be compared.

No criticism of any measurement technique or syndicated service is implied. The comparisons are made merely to illustrate the type of analysis that can be conducted to learn what specific assumptions must be made in order to accept the results of any given measurement technique.

Of course, comparisons also can be drawn among the available techniques that are so compared. Thus, a potential user can decide which methods are acceptable or unacceptable to him.

Figure 3 COMPARISONS OF IDEALIZED MEASUREMENT PROCEDURE (IMP) WITH VARIOUS ADVERTISING MEASUREMENT TECHNIQUES (July, 1967)

SEVEN BASIC ATTRIBUTES OF A MEASUREMENT TECHNIQUE	IDEALIZED MEASUREMENT PROCEDURE (IMP)	SYNDICATE			
		Audience Studies Inc. (ASI)	Gallup & Robinson Magazine Impact Service (Aided Recall)	Gallup & Robinson, Inc. Total Prime Time (TPT)	Marder Ad Evaluation Program
1. Scope of the advertising being measured:					
a. Insertions	Many	One	One	One	One
b. Media	All relevant media for planned campaign	TV	Magazine	TV	Magazine
2. Response(s) measured	Natural purchase (overtime)	Simulated purchase	Advertisement recall[1]	Advertisement recall[1]	Brand Awareness and Attitude
3. Conditions of exposure:					
a. Exposure environment	Natural	Theater	Natural	Natural	Natural
b. Advertising context	Natural	TV pilot programs out of context[1]	Natural	Natural	Natural
4. Condition of measurements:					
a. Method of data collection	Unobserved audit	Subject Questionnaire mechanical	Personal interview	Telephone interview	Telephone interview
b. Measurement environment	Natural	Awareness of test	Awareness of advertisement test	Awareness of advertisement test	Awareness of test
5. Sampling procedure:					
a. Sample element	Individual purchase unit	Individual	Individual	Individual	Individual
b. Restrictions	None	Geographic[2] Participation[3] Other[4]	Participation[2]	Geographic[2] Media[3] Participation[1]	Geographic[1] Media[2] Participation[3]
c. Method	Probability	Nonprobability[5] Quota	Nonprobability[3]	Probability	Probability
d. Size	Optional[1]	Batch (250)	Standard (400)	Standard (2,800)	Standard (4,800)
6. Type of comparison	Alternative advertisement or campaign	Norm or alternative advertisement	Norm or alternative advertisement	Norm or alternative advertisement	Alternative advertisement or campaign, and control
7. Data Handling	Unweighted	Unweighted	Weighted	Unweighted	Unweighted
	[1]Large enough so that similar results would be obtained if test were repeated	[1]In context for spot commercials seen between programs [2]Los Angeles area [3]Not all who are approached participate [4]People in high traffic centers, such as shopping centers [5]Controlled demographically	[1]Also idea recall and buying attitude [2]Not all who are contacted participate [3]Selected on a systematic basis	[1]Also idea recall and buying attitude [2]Philadelphia area [3]Viewers of program in which advertisement is placed [4]Not all who are contacted participate	[1]Subscribers in New York, Chicago, Philadelphia [2]Saturday Evening Post subscribers [3]Not all who are contacted participate

NOTE: This chart is intended to simplify comparison of syndicated and nonsyndicated measurement techniques with IMP.

However, some of the comparisons can be misleading unless the explanations and qualifications presented in Chapter III are read along with the chart. For example, each of the actual techniques and services differs in several respects from IMP. Differences between a service or technique and IMP are to be expected; whether these differences are significant to the user is something he must decide for each different application.

EXAMPLES OF MEASUREMENT TECHNIQUES

Milwaukee Advertising Laboratory	Schwerin Standard TV Testing Service	Starch Readership Service	NONSYNDICATED			
			Market Test	On-air TV Test	Psychogalvano-meter Test	Split Run Test
Many	One	One	One	One	One	Usually one
TV, newspaper, Sunday Supplement	TV	Magazine	All relevant for planned campaign	TV	All relevant for planned campaign	Newspaper or Magazine or Sunday supplement
Claimed purchase (overtime)	Simulated purchase	Advertisement recall	Usually purchase related (overtime)	Brand Preference	Physiological response[1]	Choice of several types—sales, inquiries, aware-ness, etc.
Natural	Theater	Natural	Natural	Natural	Laboratory	Natural
Natural	TV pilot programs	Natural	Natural	Natural	Often out of context	Natural
Subject diary	Subject Questionnaire	Personal interview	Audit or diary	Telephone interview	Mechanical recording	Personal interview or subject response
Awareness of test	Awareness of test	Awareness of advertisement test	Natural	Awareness of test	Laboratory	Awareness of test
Family	Individual	Individual	Reselling Organization (store)	Individual	Individual	Individual or family
Geographic[1] Media[2] Participation[3]	Geographic Participation[2]	Media[1] Participation[2]	Geographic[1] Participation[2]	Geographic[1] Media[2] Participation[3]	Participation[2]	Media[1] Participation[2]
Nonprobability[1]	Probability	Nonprobability[3]	Probability	Probability	Nonprobability[3]	Probability
Standard (1,500)[5]	Batch (300 to 700)[3]	Standard (200-300)	Optional	Optional	Optional	Optional
Alternative advertisement or campaign, and control	Norm or alternative advertisement	Norm or alternative advertisement	Goal	Norm	Alternative advertisement	Alternative advertisement or control
Unweighted	Weighted	Unweighted	Unweighted	Unweighted	Unweighted	Unweighted
[1]Milwaukee [2]Milwaukee Journal subscribers [3]Limited per-cent agree to join panel [4]Panel controlled demographic-ally [5]Another 750 family panel is available	[1]Usually New York or Chicago, occasion-ally other cities [2]Not all who are contacted participate [3]Average audience in N.Y.C. is 300; in Chicago, 600 to 700	[1]Readers of vehicle in which advertisement is run [2]Not all who are contacted participate [3]Selection based on a quota	[1]Generally limited to relatively few markets [2]Stores willing to participate usually limited	[1]Generally limited to relatively few markets [2]Viewers of the show in which adver-tisement is placed [3]Not all who are contacted participate	[1]Galvanic skin response [2]Generally done in a laboratory which often deters participants [3]Usually	[1]Readers of vehicle in which split is run [2]Not all who are contacted participate

THE SEVEN BASIC ATTRIBUTES OF
MEASUREMENT TECHNIQUES

The following discussion regarding the seven basic attributes of measurement techniques relates specifically to the seven attributes listed in the overall chart.

1. Scope of the Advertising Being Measured

Techniques for measuring advertising effectiveness vary with regard to the scope of the advertising they are capable of evaluating. Some techniques, such as market tests, are capable of assessing effects of an entire advertising campaign, using different advertisements and a varying number of insertions, in virtually any media.

Examples include the technique used by the Milwaukee Advertising Laboratory and certain split-run tests. In contrast, a large number of techniques are designed to measure the effects of a single advertisement, for example, those used by the Starch Readership Service and the Schwerin Standard TV Testing Service.

Hence, the scope of the advertising that a technique is capable of evaluating may be described partially by specifying whether single or multiple insertions are involved and the medium or media that can be used. A technique that uses multiple insertions can assess the effects of repetitive insertions of the same advertisement or a number of insertions of different advertisements. Thus, the capacity to handle multiple insertions is crucial to the assessment of advertising campaigns as such. Ideally, in order to measure the effects of alternative content or alternative media in advertising campaigns, one would need the capacity to include entire campaigns in the measure.

The scope of the advertising that the Idealized Measurement Procedure should be capable of assessing is a complete advertising campaign, encompassing multiple insertions in virtually all media. Advertising measurement techniques frequently are used

TABLE 3.1

Advertising Unit	Insertions	Media	Example
Unrestricted Campaign	Multiple	Unrestricted	Market Test
Restricted Campaign	Multiple	Two or more, but restricted	Milwaukee Advertising Laboratory
Single Medium Campaign	Multiple	One	Split-run
Advertisement	Single	One	Starch Readership Service

to evaluate alternative advertising campaigns. In Table 3.1, the advertising attributes which actual advertising measurement techniques measure are ranked in terms of closeness to IMP.

Any technique that has the capacity to assess an advertising attribute at a given level also can be used to assess advertising attributes at a "lower" level, although to do so would be in general, wasteful. As an example, a market test could be used to measure the effects of a single insertion of an advertisement but is unlikely to be used in that way.

2. Response(s) Measured

It is well recognized that advertising can effect a number of measurable phenomena in a market. One of the most important ways in which advertising measurement techniques differ is in the aspect of the market's behavior chosen to reflect the effects of the advertising.

Likely, *the ultimate criterion of relative advertising effectiveness would be the present value (today's dollar equivalents) of the relative profitability of advertising alternatives.* To arrive at such a measure, IMP would have to assume some response to the advertising which is directly translatable into profit terms.

The proposed ideal unit of response is an *individual's purchase of the product or services advertised, or related products or services.* With histories of the purchase patterns of individuals associated with the various advertising alternatives, along with the incremental costs of the items purchased and their prices, there exists sufficient economic theory to deduce the relative contribution to profits of differences in purchase patterns.

Some techniques focus on purchases, or the sales associated with purchases, and may employ measures such as factory shipments, store sales, purchase diaries, coupon redemption, or actual observed purchases to reflect the effectiveness of advertising. Market tests, for example, usually use purchases or sales to reflect advertising's effects.

Most advertising measurement techniques, however, use people's verbal responses to gauge advertising's effects. These responses may be separated into responses regarding the product or brand, and those regarding the advertising itself.

The hierarchy-of-effects theory, discussed in Chapter II (p. 20) offers a framework for classifying the kinds of communications responses to the product or brand which are used as indicators of effectiveness.

Measures of conviction generally include simulated purchases and intentions to buy. A simulated purchase is a situation in which the subject chooses a brand or product which he believes he will receive, or at least has a chance to receive, and in which no commitment of the subject's own money is involved. The response utilized by the Schwerin Standard TV Testing Service is an example of a simulated purchase.

Another class of responses that is often used to gauge the effectiveness of advertising is the extent to which attitudes toward the product are influenced by advertising. These attitudes are usually reflected in the liking of, or a stated preference for, the product or brand advertised. One of the responses of the Marder Ad Evaulation Program is a preference measure for the advertised brand.

Another response used frequently to measure the effects of advertising is the amount of knowledge people have of the brand or product. The extent to which the basic message of the advertising has been "learned" is often the response sought.

Finally, awareness of the existence of the brand or product is often used as an indicator of effect. Awareness measures include a range of responses. "Top-of-the-mind" awareness is the extent to which people name the brand first, spontaneously. "Unaided" awareness is the ability to name the brand at all, without prompting. "Aided" awareness is the extent to which respondents express familiarity with the brand when it is suggested to them.

In addition to verbal responses concerning the product or brand, verbal responses concerning a particular advertisement or advertising campaign are often used as indicators of advertising effects. For example, the ability to play back or recall the theme or key slogan of a campaign is often used.

For specific advertisements, people's ability to recall whether or not they have been exposed often is utilized as a measure of effect in post measures. Examples of services using this type of measure include the Starch Readership Service and both the Gallup & Robinson Magazine Impact Service and Total Prime Time for television.

Finally, some researchers have experimented with responses that are neither purchase nor verbal responses to advertising. Rather they are physical or physiological. The physical responses are generally based on the notion that the amount of effort a person is voluntarily willing to exert is a measure of the reward he is getting for his effort. Using special apparatus, people are exposed to advertising and made to exert effort, such as repeatedly pushing a pedal, to see and/or hear the advertising. The amount of effort they exert, then, is a measure of their "reward," which in turn reflects an effect of the advertising.

Physiological responses are involuntary bodily reactions of people considered to reflect true emotional responses to stimuli. Since they bypass language and are involuntary, deception on the part of the respondent is unlikely. Examples of physiological responses that have been used to reflect advertising effects are electrical skin resistance (in the psychogalvanometer), the dilation of the pupil of the eye, and salivation.

3. Conditions of Exposure

For advertising to have an effect, people obviously must be exposed to it. The conditions under which the exposure takes place may be outlined by describing, first, the physical environment in which the person is exposed to the advertising, and second, the context or "editorial environment" in which the advertising is exposed.

In an ideal measure, the people should be exposed naturally to the advertising, in their homes or offices, without artifacts of any sort. Similarly, the advertisements ideally should appear within the natural context of the media in which they would be used — commercials inset in the shows in which they would appear, print advertisements in their respective magazines and newspapers, and so on for other advertising.

In the post measurement of effectiveness, by definition the advertising has appeared naturally and people have or have not been exposed naturally. In some advertising pretests, such as on-air tests and split-runs in print media, natural conditions of exposure obtain as well.

However, in some pretests, conditions are used which deviate from the natural. The exposure environment of some pretests may be described as "laboratories." Movie theater pretests of television commercials are perhaps the best example. In addition, where special equipment is involved, as in the physical or physiological measures, the exposures usually have to take place in advertising research laboratories of one sort or another.

There are also pretests of advertising in which the exposure is in the subject's home but artificially simulated. For example, a TV commercial pretest in which the subject sees the commercial via a rear screen projector in the home could not be considered a perfectly natural exposure environment.

A number of deviations from the ideal also occur with respect to the advertising context in which the exposure occurs. For one, the medium of presentation may not be the one in which the advertisement would appear if actually used as intended. Examples include the use of large screen movies and rear screen projectors to test TV commercials, and slide presentations to test print advertisements or outdoor posters.

A second deviation concerns the "editorial" context of the advertising. A TV commercial to be used in a dramatic presentation or in a news program may be tested in a comedy, or a magazine advertisement to be used in a women's service magazine may be tested in a general weekly, as is done in the Marder Ad Evaluation Program. Some advertising is tested out of any editorial context. For example, the Audience Studies, Inc., TV commercial pretesting technique does not embed the commercial being tested within the context of a show.

4. Conditions of Measurement

In order to develop a numerical measure of the relative effectiveness of the advertising alternatives, one must decide not only what aspect of people's behavior or of the market's behavior will be the critical response, but also how this behavior will be observed and recorded. The conditions of measurement must take into account the method of data collection and the measurement environment, particularly the extent to which the measurement process makes the subjects aware that they are involved in a test.

Ideally, one would observe subjects' responses directly without their being aware that they are under observation or involved in a measurement process. Since the ideal response to be observed is the actual purchase pattern of individuals, one must conceive of the ideal standard as a process of secret, direct observation of the purchases of the people involved. Clearly such a process is usually impossible to execute.

Nevertheless, it remains the ideal against which all other processes are to be compared. This problem is analogous to the technician's problem in measuring voltage and currents in an electronic circuit. Unless a suitable instrument is employed (such as a vacuum-tube voltmeter) the meter itself will impose such a load on the circuit being measured that severe distortion will result and no meaningful measurement will be obtained. While one does not need perfect instruments, they still have to be tolerable by the system being tested in order to yield meaningful results.

Methods for obtaining data on responses to advertising vary widely, depending mainly upon the performance criterion being measured. Sales data can be obtained through store audits or factory shipments. Results also are obtainable through purchase diaries, pantry checks, direct responses for mail order and, occasionally, even direct observation.

Communications measures can be obtained through personal and telephone interviews as well as self-administered questionnaires either delivered through the mail or distributed to a group. Coupon returns and "bingo" cards requesting information are also used to measure advertising's effects.

Finally, observation and recording of physical and physiological measures are usually accomplished by the use of special automatic equipment designed for the purpose.

Most measures are impossible to obtain without the subject being aware that he is being observed in some way. The only practicable exceptions are such indirect measures as store audits and factory shipments. However, in many of the techniques, the subjects realize they are involved in some sort of measurement process but do not know that the measures have anything to do with advertising.

5. Sampling Procedures

The sampling of people whose responses will be used to gauge the advertising's effects obviously will have an effect on the advertising's ratings. The sampling procedure has four parts:

1. *The Sample Attribute* — The basic unit which is to be observed, usually an individual but not always.
2. *Restrictions* — Most techniques restrict rather severely the portion of the population who have any chance at all of appearing in the sample of people to be observed.
3. *Method* — The method of choosing the specific people to participate in the measure.
4. *Size* — The total number of people on which the final measure is usually based.

As an ideal standard for the sampling process, this report proposes a very large unrestricted probability sample drawn from the entire population. The size would be such that the measurement error would be very small compared with the expected differences in effectiveness among the advertising alternatives.

In practice, samples frequently deviate in a number of ways from the ideal. While the vast majority of advertising measurement techniques utilizes the individual as the sample attribute, some use the family (as in certain purchase diaries), the retail outlet (in store audits), or a geographical area (in factory shipments).

Rarely is a sample unrestricted. Usually, the participants are drawn from a single or limited number of geographic areas which were chosen systematically on the basis of cost or convenience. Aside from geographic restrictions, a number of measurement techniques draw respondents from the audience or readership of a single medium. An example of a media restriction appears in the Marder Ad Evaluation Program, which uses only *Saturday Evening Post* subscribers.

Given the restrictions in the sampling process, the methods by which the actual samples are drawn from the eligible population vary widely. Entire books have been written on the sampling process, and no attempt can be made here to explore the subject in depth. Suffice it to say that a number of techniques use essentially random or probability type samples, others employ quota samples, and still others use systematic samples.

It is probably true that both art and science are required for drawing a truly representative sample. A nonrepresentative sample can lead to disastrous conclusions. Yet size of sample alone does not ensure projectability of results. Then, as the heterogeneity of the population being sampled increases, so must the sample become correspondingly larger in order to reflect the many characteristics of market segments observed.

Sample size usually is predetermined in the syndicated services, and optional in the application of the other measurement techniques. In the pretesting syndicated services, however, the test may be repeated a number of times so that some control exists on sample size.

Another restriction becomes serious when an appreciable number of those selected to participate do not do so due to the difficulty in reaching them or their unwillingness to cooperate. Various techniques differ with respect to the extent to which such restrictions apply to them.

6. Type of Comparison

As already indicated, we are considering only the concept of *relative* advertising effectiveness. Any technique which purports to measure relative effectiveness presupposes the capacity to compare the "scores" achieved by alternatives. The ideal standard, represented by IMP, would be a technique which permitted simultaneous direct comparisons of a large number of advertising alternatives.

In the previous section, the ideal sample was described as a very large unrestricted probability sample drawn from the entire population. Ideally, a sample of this sort would be drawn for each of the advertising alternatives and the advertising associated with each alternative would be exposed only to its respective sample. Hence, in the ideal situation the purchases made by that sample would reflect the effects only of that advertising alternative.

Although few pretests of advertising provide for direct comparison of alternatives as an inherent part of the technique, most can be so used by testing the alternatives at different times. One technique that does provide for direct comparison of two alternatives is the Marder Ad Evaluation Program.

Often, the score received by an advertising alternative is compared to a "norm" or average rather than another alternative. For example, the Schwerin Standard TV Testing Service generally provides "norms" for product classes for which many commercials have been tested. Of course, such average measures can be faulted, but they are often intuitively appealing and possess stability.

Some techniques provide for a comparison of results with a

control group which has not been exposed to any of the alternatives in question. The television portion of the Milwaukee Advertising Laboratory, for example, provides the capability of cutting out a TV campaign from a portion of the panel.

Some post-measures of advertising's effect also provide norms against which to compare the scores received by an advertisement. Both Starch and Gallup & Robinson provide such norms for their respective techniques.

Sometimes the performance of advertising is assessed by comparing some measure of performance with a predetermined goal for the advertising. In this approach there is no attempt to establish relative performance.

7. Data Handling

Finally, the data gathered by observing the responses of the sample to the advertising must be processed in some way, so as to arrive at the final measure or score for each advertising alternative.

In the IMP standard, the relevant purchases made by each individual in each sample in each time period would be tabulated. These data would have to be translated into the present value of the relative contributions to profit of each of the advertising alternatives.

To do this, data on the incremental profits to the advertiser of each product in each time period would be needed, as well as the advertising costs in each time period. With such data, the differences in patterns of purchases associated with the advertising alternatives could be translated into the relative contributions to profit associated with each of the advertising alternatives. These values would be discounted and summed to a single present value, to arrive at the relative dollar profit effectiveness of each of the alternatives.

In contrast to this ideal, most of the techniques used for measuring advertising effects simply tabulate their raw data into the scores they present. The scores, then, depend only on the data actually gathered in the course of the measure.

Some techniques, in order to make up for possible demographic imbalances among their participants or for other reasons, weight the original raw data differentially. These weights usually depend on data other than that gathered for the measurement of effectiveness.

SOME IMPLICATIONS

In this chapter a framework has been developed for analyzing techniques for measuring advertising effectiveness. An Idealized

Measurement Procedure (IMP) has been developed, consisting of a standard of seven idealized attributes. To the extent that any actual advertising measurement technique deviates from this idealized standard, with respect to one or more attributes, some concessions must be made in the form of compromise assumptions if the technique is to be applied and used as a basis for decisions. These assumptions have the effect of allowing for deficiencies in available techniques versus the ideal.

The seven attributes if IMP can be focused on two dimensions of measurement techniques—the dimensions of *context* and that of *environmental measurement factors.* The first dimension consists of the first two attributes—the *scope* of the advertising being measured and the *response(s)* measured. The second dimension incorporates the conditions of *exposure,* the conditions of *measurement, sampling procedure,* type of *comparison,* and *data handling.* Given this classification, the following discussion of the assumptions concerning deviations from each of the attributes of IMP is divided into two chapters—IV and V.

One may conceive of the *results* of applying IMP to a pair of advertising alternatives as what one would ideally like to mean by the "relative advertising effectiveness" of those advertising alternatives. Of course, IMP is an ideal and, like most ideals, is probably unrealizable in practice; yet it serves as a recognizable target and an idealized standard of excellence towards which to strive.

Nevertheless, the speculative results of IMP's application still may be conceived of as being what one means when discussing the relative effectiveness of advertising. With such a standard in mind, differences of opinion as to which of a number of techniques "really" measures advertising effectiveness may be reduced to researchable questions, such as "which of the techniques contains the fewest, or most acceptable, assumptions?"

There may still be disagreements; but the disagreements are more likely to be on the interpretation of facts or restrictions, rather than on illusive semantic differences or emotional claims.

IV

Assumptions Concerning the Scope of Advertising and Responses Measured

CAREFUL EXAMINATION of the *assumptions* underlying the various techniques for measuring advertising effectiveness is an important factor. After all, these assumptions represent what one must be prepared to accept in using any measurement technique or model. And the time for considering these assumptions is *before,* and not after, the commitment of resources for any measurement program.

The analysis in the previous chapter of IMP and of various actual measurement techniques reveals numerous differences. It follows that these differences should be accounted for, if the results of any technique are going to be used effectively in connection with decision making about advertising.

Typically the user of measurement techniques evaluates them by listing their advantages and disadvantages, and then trying to integrate this information into an overall judgmental rating. Such a procedure requires him to make some general approximations, to satisfy himself that the results are likely to be related to his advertising objectives.

In contrast, the proposed new framework of analysis enables the user to break down each measurement technique into its basic factors and to make point-by-point comparisons with the elements of the two major parts of IMP: The Response Measured and the Environmental Factors and Techniques of Measurement. Each point of difference requires him to recognize some assumptions to justify deviations from IMP. After examining these assumptions, the user can then assess the relative strength and importance of each of them.

Hopefully, this new framework will enable the user to examine more closely the specific assumptions inherent in his choice of a measurement technique. And hopefully it will lead to better choices of measurement techniques, and thereby to better advertising decisions.

A comparison between current practice and use of the Idealized Measurement Procedure for estimating the validity and reliability of advertising measurement techniques is presented schematically in Figure 4.1.

FIGURE 4.1

Current Practice Versus IMP for Evaluating
Advertising Measurement Techniques

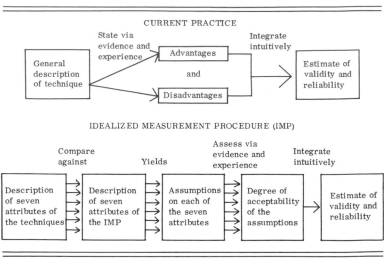

CONDITIONS OF ACCEPTABILITY

The following discussion relates to the overall conditions which must be met in order to make any of the measures of advertising effectiveness useful for decision making among equal cost advertising alternatives.

The acceptance or rejection of an assumption may be based upon any of three factors:

1. Proved general principles regarding the assumed relationship—as from empirical studies in psychology and communications.
2. Specific evidence supporting or countering the assumption.
3. Advertising judgment.

Unfortunately there are few proved general principles in advertising, and only limited pieces of specific evidence bearing on the nature of the assumptions underlying the use of measurement techniques. Therefore, the acceptance or rejection of the assumptions usually has been based primarily on judgment.

When such judgment is directed to explicitly stated assumptions concerning the seven factors of the techniques, this should result in better subjective estimates of the validity and reliability of measurement techniques than currently are obtained.

In this chapter and the following the seven elements of the Idealized Measurement Procedure will be reexamined and compared further with existing measurement techniques. The assumptions that must be made in order to justify the deviations of current techniques from the IMP standard will be stated. If strong evidence for or against these assumptions exists, the nature of this evidence will be highlighted.

In addition to providing a framework for the evaluation of advertising measurement techniques, comparison with IMP can also provide a guide for future research and development. At points where certain assumptions appear crucial yet evidence and experience are weak, additional research to test those assumptions might be in order. In carrying out such research, advertisers might demonstrate that some assumptions have little real importance. Other assumptions, although important, might be accepted on the basis of intuitively appealing evidence about the nature of the link between the factors involved.

Similarly, the evidence might suggest that some assumptions are so crucial that the measurement technique either must be replaced by a more appropriate one or revised so as to reduce the gap between the actual and the ideal elements.

Consider a number of advertising alternatives to be rated by an advertising measurement technique. Assume that one of the advertising alternatives is, in fact, truly the most effective. That is, if the relative effectiveness of all alternatives could be measured against the Idealized Measurement Procedure, this one would be best, another second best, etc.

The overall validity of any advertising measurement technique can be related to how well the ranking of the alternatives by that technique would compare with their "true" rank, that is, the ranking that would be obtained if the alternatives were measured by IMP. Actual measurement techniques vary from near perfect to woefully inadequate.

A perfect measurement technique would always rank alternative advertisements in exactly the same order as the idealized procedure. A good technique obviously would almost always rank as "best" an advertising alternative that was truly among the best of the alternatives. Where there were only two alternatives, it would usually rank the better one higher. A barely adequate technique more often than not would rank as "best" an advertising alternative that was truly average or better in effectiveness. With only two alternatives, it would rank the better one higher only a little over half the time.

A technique with no validity would be just as likely to rank a below average alternative as "best" as it would an alternative that was above average. These conditions are illustrated in Figure 4.2.

FIGURE 4. 2

A Sampling of Hypothetical Techniques Versus IMP
Illustrating Varying Degrees of Validity
in Ranking Advertising Alternatives

Advertising alternatives	IMP ranking	Typical Ranking Produced by a			
		Perfect technique	Good technique	"Adequate" technique	Invalid technique
C	1	1	2	3	5
A	2	2	1	1	3
E	3	3	3	5	2
F	4	4	5	4	6
B	5	5	4	6	1
D	6	6	6	2	4

A measure of the similarity of two rankings of the same set of objects is the rank correlation between them. If the ranking of the alternatives with respect to their scores on the measurement technique tends to have a high positive rank correlation with their ranking by the IMP, this would satisfy the conditions for a good measurement technique. A perfect one-to-one correspondence of ranks would yield a coefficient of correlation of one. If no agreement were present, then the coefficient would be zero.

An inverse ranking of IMP scores versus the actual technique would be expressed as a negative coefficient of correlation of minus one (a most unlikely situation). A technique having a high rank correlation with the Idealized Measurement Procedure would be more likely to rate as "best" a truly superior advertising alternative than would a technique with a lower rank correlation.

To the extent that a measurement technique differs from IMP with respect to one or more factors, one would expect that the ranking of alternatives resulting from that measure would deviate from the ranking which would result from the use of IMP. The nature and extent of such anticipated deviations should relate to the rank correlation which would exist between the technique and IMP. The more important the factors that deviate and the greater the deviations, the lower would be the expected rank correlation.

Hence, the basic assumption that has to be made in order not to reject a technique on the basis of a deviation in a particular factor is that this deviation alone would *not* lower the rank correlation to unacceptably low levels.

THE BASIC ASSUMPTIONS

The remainder of this chapter, and all of the following chapter, is devoted to a searching analysis of the *assumptions* that underlie the various measurement techniques. This means that the seven basic attributes already described in Chapter III are now considered one by one as to the theories or assumptions involved.

Since the assumptions concerning the two context attributes are the most critical ones from the user's point of view, they are to be analyzed next—followed by an analysis in Chapter V of the additional five attributes.

1. Scope of the Advertising Being Measured

The scope of the advertising activity that the hypothetical IMP technique might ''handle'' is an entire advertising campaign, including multiple insertions of different advertisements in different media. Contemporary advertising measurement techniques deviate from this IMP ideal in one basic way—most of them attempt to estimate the effectiveness of an entire campaign by measuring effects produced from a particular portion of the campaign.

The portion used may be the bulk of the campaign—as, for example, when a campaign consists of 90 percent prime time television and only 10 percent print media. In such a situation, evaluating the entire campaign may be quite adequate by measuring only the relative effects of the television portion. On the other hand, campaign decisions sometimes are based on a mere fragment of the campaign, for instance, when alternative campaigns are evaluated by measuring the effects of only a single ''representative'' advertisement from each.

It may be perfectly appropriate for a portion of a campaign to be used for assessing the success of an entire campaign. As stated previously, the basic requisite to have validity is that the ranking of the ''sample'' portion of the campaign correspond to its actual ranking, or to that which would obtain if the entire campaign were measured by the IMP method.

To examine the underlying factors which could prevent this condition from being met, three kinds of deviations from the ideal should be explored:

1. Using a single advertisement or commercial, or a small number of these, to generalize on the effects of the complete set of advertisements and/or commercials associated with a campaign.
2. Using a single exposure, or a small number of them, to generalize on the effects of repeated exposures over time for the campaign.
3. Using the effects of advertising out of a media context in a single vehicle or in a small number of vehicles to generalize on the effects of the advertising in the complete set of media and vehicles associated with the campaign.

FIGURE 4.3

The Three Key Assumptions Underlying the
Scope of the Advertising Being Tested

Test	Single or limited advertise- ment	Single or limited insertions	One or limited vehicle	
	Infer 1 on	Infer 2 on	Infer 3	
Campaign	class of advertise- ment	multiple insertions	multiple vehicle within the medium	Other media

These situations exclude measurement techniques designed for concept testing [1] or for measurement of part of an advertisement, such as its headlines, captions, illustrations, and so forth. The reason for this exclusion is that most techniques which are able to handle a finished advertisement can also be used for concept and advertising component testing.

Hence, the problems associated with measurement of a single advertisement exist also for the concept and component testing; clearly the user should be aware of the possible limitations as well as potential benefits of these testing procedures. This indicates that care must be exercised to see that the hidden assumptions or "assumption structure" underlying the use of the techniques can be accepted, just as many sweet sugar-coated pills have a bitter core. The surface appeals of many testing techniques must be reconciled with some sobering limitations and even distressing weaknesses that accompany their use.

The three deviations concerning the scope of the advertisement are summarized schematically in Figure 4.3.

Not all techniques for measuring advertising effectiveness require the three assumptions above. For example, certain measuring techniques such as market tests are capable of handling an unlimited number of insertions in an unlimited number of media. They correspond to the IMP ideal in this respect and, therefore, need no moderating assumptions.

However, if the scope of the advertising being measured is not an unrestricted campaign, the foregoing three assumptions have to be made. Moreover, the closer the scope of the advertising being measured to an unrestricted campaign, such as used in the IMP method, the weaker the assumptions needed to accept the technique as adequate.

The three assumptions indicated in Figure 4.3 focus on the need to make evaluations concerning whole campaigns based on results measured from portions of the campaign. There is no conclusive empirical or theoretical evidence as to the validity of these assumptions. In fact, there are some reasons to doubt their validity.

Concerning *the inference from a single or limited advertisement to a whole class of advertisements,* it is not very likely that a campaign will consist only of multiple insertions of a single advertisement.

There are numerous advertising and communication studies that highlight the positive effects of a variety of messages (different advertisements) on the audience's response. Yet a large number of measurment techniques test only single or limited advertisements.

This situation leads to the assumption that the difference in effectiveness between a selected advertisement and the other advertisements of the same campaign tends to be smaller than the difference in effectiveness between advertisements of two distinct campaigns.

Concerning the inference from a single or limited insertion to multiple insertions, it is conceivable that there are situations in which advertisement A, which represents campaign A, will rank higher than B, which represents campaign B, in a pretest using single or limited insertions, but with the campaign of advertisement B more effective.

For example, if advertisement B is less believable than advertisement A, it might score poorly in the pretest, but due to a "sleeper" effect[2] it may perform better than A in a multiple insertion situation. The empirical evidence on the relationship between single and multiple insertions is far from being conclusive, however, and research is needed to establish the validity of this assumption.

The *assumption concerning the media element of the advertising being measured* applies to two distinct situations.

First, it applies to the case where the inference from a test to the real world is done within a single medium. For example, a measuring technique may handle advertisements in a weekly magazine, and at the same time the "real world" campaign may be designed to run *only* in magazines.

Second, it applies to the case where inter-media inferences are required. For example, from a test of TV commercials to a combined TV, radio, and print campaign, with no conclusive empirical evidence concerning the media assumption, it is easier to accept "intuitively" the intra-media inferences than the inter-media inferences. The latter requires at least some empirical evidence, since if accepted it implies that the medium itself does not effect the rank of audience response. (No differences are assumed between audience, since this is taken care of by the sampling assumption.) There are a number of studies, however, that emphasize the effect of media on the final response.

Consequently, these three assumptions or any combination

subset thereof must be made for the appropriate measuring technique. A careful review of pertinent published materials reveals no conclusive empirical evidence that either refutes or supports these assumptions. Numerous studies have been conducted on the effects of repetition of advertisements, multiple media advertising, and so forth; but none of these studies has any direct relevance to the above assumptions.

Hence, in using techniques that are restricted with regard to the scope of the advertising being measured, the advertiser today has to rely primarily on his judgment, coupled with whatever experience he and others have gained.

2.   Responses Measured

As illustrated in the previous chapter, advertising effects can be measured in a variety of ways. These measured responses can be clarified, for the purpose of evaluating techniques for measuring advertising effectiveness, into two basic categories: (1) *purchase responses* and (2) *nonpurchase responses.*

Ideally, relative advertising effectiveness should be measured by the net improvements or differential effects of the advertising alternatives on people's purchasing behavior. The use of any technique which uses a response other than purchases by the individuals requires assumptions on the relationship between the response measured and purchase behavior. These assumptions, whether on the direct or indirect link between the response measured and the ideal response specified by IMP, follow the pattern of the basic assumption on the relation between the attributes of a technique and the attributes of IMP.

a. *Measures of Purchase Responses.* In certain situations purchase responses of individuals to advertising alternatives can be measured directly. Mail-order houses, for example, can compare the differential effectiveness of two or more advertising alternatives by keeping track of actual purchase results. It is obvious that no compromise assumptions have to be made, since the actual response measured and the ideal suggested by IMP are identical.

Other techniques, such as market tests which use consumer panel data based on purchase diaries, require no strong assumptions since the recorded response measured is usually a good approximation to the ideal measure of what really occurs. One does have to assume, though, that the accuracy in recording of purchases has not been distorted by the different advertising alternatives.

On the other hand, use of factory shipments or retail orders as measures of purchase response requires a slightly stronger assumption concerning the link between the response and the purchases of the ultimate buyers. A difference in effect on inventories at the wholesale and retail levels and on the time lag of their responses to consumer demand could alter the apparent ranking of the alternatives.

b. *Measures of Nonpurchase Responses.* Recognition, recall, and association tests; opinion and attitude ratings; physiological tests; and sales inquiries are only some of the more common measures of nonpurchase responses used in measuring advertising effectiveness. An operational classification of these and other existing measures is the following:

1. *Marketing search actions* — such as inquiries, shopping behavior, search for information
2. *Verbal responses* — such as awareness, attitude
3. *Internal (physiological) responses*
4. *Physical responses*

Although often classification schemes are feasible, the rationale for the above grouping is that the structure for all members of a given category is similar. Moreover, the similarities of measures within a category apparently are greater than the similarities of measures of two distinct categories.

(1) *Marketing Search Actions.* The number of inquiries an advertisement produces is used in some split-run pretests, and sometimes as a post measure of advertising effectiveness.

This use of inquiries assumes that an advertisement producing more inquiries will also produce more sales. There is no conclusive evidence on the relationship between inquiries and actual purchase behavior. Often a more selective advertisement will produce fewer inquiries, but more relevant ones. Furthermore, a Starch study comparing Starch scores on noting and reading with inquiries resulting from advertisements revealed no consistent relationship between them.

In commenting on inquiries as a measure, Darrell B. Lucas and Steuart Henderson Britt emphasize some of the problems:

> Generalized interpretations of the meaning of a large volume of responses from a coupon are complicated by the fact that most consumers *never* clip any magazine coupon. They prefer to consult other sources for information or to buy and try new products. The readers of some publications are extremely unresponsive to coupon offers, although they may prove excellent customers. There are also seasonal differences in coupon returns for most products, as well as general seasonal differences in coupon flow — February and October normally bring much higher responses than June and December. Economic slumps are likely to stimulate responses to free offers, and new products may bring more inquiries than well-established ones. When these and other factors are added to the variable influence of the specific offer,

there can be little justification for projecting a few thousand inquiries to the response of the whole audience of an advertisement. Nor can the effectiveness of advertising media be safely judged on this basis alone. [2*]

Until further evidence is available on the relationships between inquiries or any other nonpurchase marketing response (such as shopping behavior) and actual purchase behavior, advertisers should be fully aware of the fact that an advertisement that produces more nonpurchase marketing response than another does not necessarily lead to more sales.

(2) *Verbal Responses.* Recognition, recall, association, and attitude are all measures of verbal response to advertisements. Similarly, awareness and attitude measures are used to gauge people's responses toward the product, brand, or institution advertised. The rationale for using these and other verbal responses as measures of advertising effectiveness is embodied in the hierarchy-of-effects or correlates-of-effects assumptions (see Chapter II).

The flow of cause-and-effect relationship between any of these measures and sales may be in either direction—from awareness to buying, or from buying to awareness. Although there is no conclusive empirical evidence supporting a causal relationship between awareness of either the product or the advertisement and sales, there is some evidence to indicate a correlation between both these measures and sales. Not all of the evidence indicates a positive correlation, however. It can be negative as well, for example, a higher recall score can be associated with either higher or lower sales.

The idea underlying the hierarchy-of-effects concept is that, in general, buyers move through a sequence of stages of a buying continuum, starting with exposure to the advertising and culminating with a final purchase. While this thinking is reflected in many important ways by managers and researchers alike, there is no general consensus as to the precise number of stages and their nature. For example, the National Industrial Conference Board proposed the following five-stage hierarchy:

1. Creation of an awareness of the product in the mind of the potential buyer.
2. Nurturing an acceptance for the product.
3. Establishing a preference for the product.
4. Arousing an interest to buy the product, and
5. Provoking the sale. [3]

[2*] From, *Measuring Advertising Effectiveness* by Darrell Blaine Lucas and Steuart Henderson Britt. Copyright 1963 by McGraw-Hill Book Co., Inc. Used with permission.

Robert J. Lavidge, President of the marketing research firm of Elrick and Lavidge, Inc., and the late Gary A. Steiner of the University of Chicago, suggested a model with the following sequence of stages:

1. Unawareness of the product
2. Awareness
3. Knowledge
4. Liking
5. Preference
6. Conviction
7. Purchase [4]

Russell H. Colley, who has had a marked influence on interest in the hierarchy-of-effects approach with his DAGMAR book, proposed four levels of understanding that carry a prospect from unawareness to action (purchase) through:

1. Awareness
2. Comprehension
3. Conviction
4. Action [5]

Similarly, the so-called AIDA and AIDCA formulas for copy structure are based on the hierarchy notion that an advertisement should stimulate the audience's:

A – Attention
I – Interest
D – Desire
C – Conviction
A – Action

Writers differ as to the number and nature of the stages in the buying continuum and as to the extent to which the lower stages are necessary conditions for the final buying stage. Yet, there seems to be agreement that the purchase is the culmination of several previous stages of the buying process, and that as an individual moves through the hierarchical stages, he is more likely to become a buyer.

Hence, this hierarchy-of-effects approach for measuring advertising effects is based on the assumption that each step in the hierarchy contributes to an increased probability of purchase. The assumption is a plausible one, and for that reason it seems to be accepted uncritically by some advertising people. "For if it is true that a one-way flow of progresssion from message reception to overt behavior exists, then sales as a criterion of effectiveness can be dispensed with and 'substitute' variables used instead." [6]

The use of intermediate responses – awareness, attitude, and the like—as predictors of purchase behavior, however, is valid only if some relationship is known to exist between certain stages in the hierarchy and actual purchase behavior. Without sufficient evidence on this linkage, any inference about the purchase response from measurements of the various stages in the hierarchy is unfounded. The hierarchy-of-effects theory would imply a causal linkage, whereas the correlates-of-effects theory would imply alternative assumption of a correlation measure.

But what do we really know about the specific relationships among the various stages of the hierarchical buying process? Have the relationships between attitude and subsequent purchase behavior, for example, been established?

Actually, little is known today about these issues. Even the assumption of a hierarchy has been questioned. Based on an extensive search of the literature and an examination of two specific studies of advertising effects, one researcher concludes that ". . . with one exception, there is no good evidence that such changes in awareness precede rather than follow purchase." [7] A similar conclusion has been drawn regarding the relationship between knowledge, recall, and recognition, and buying behavior.

Noting the considerable number of methodological problems bearing on the assumption of hierarchical effects, quite apart from the substantive objections, the following question has been asked.

> Is it, on balance, really more difficult and expensive to investigate the direct link between advertising expenditure and sales than it is to undertake research into each step of the hierarchy —*even if the existence of a hierarchy of effects were actually established?* [8]

The implication of the communications-goal approach (Colley) is that if communications goals are attained, progress is made in the direction of sales. During interviews carried out as a background for the present book, critics of the communications-goal-setting procedure called attention to the difficulty of establishing a realistic relationship between communications goals and marketing or corporate goals.

Although they agreed that advertising goals stated in communications terms are more readily measurable than are sales goals for advertising, they saw problems in relating a communications goal to a corporate goal expressed in dollars, or even to a marketing goal expressed in market share or sales volume terms.

The research director of one important advertising agency said, "The DAGMAR type of communications goal may be feasible, but it is useful only for the corporate image type of advertising." Another agency research executive said that there is ". . . little impact of the DAGMAR approach. Advertising goals, if any are set, are usually qualitative; and there is no systematic attempt in most cases to evaluate advertising results in terms of its goals."

Joseph E. Bachelder, Managing Director of the Marketing Communications Research Center, questions an assumption which ". . . perhaps unjustly underlies DAGMAR. The assumption is that communications as a process and a science is relatively simple. Communication is the most complex of all social sciences—yet it lies at the heart of marketing." [9]

Seymour Smith, who heads his own marketing research firm, states in discussing the assumption implicit in the DAGMAR communications spectrum that:

> . . . a prospect can be massaged through from unawareness to conviction like so much stuffing in a sausage. Obviously, some sales follow this classic path described by the DAGMAR communications spectrum. In fact, enough sales are made in this pattern to give the whole thing an aura of realism. All sales do not follow the simple path outlined in the DAGMAR spectrum. The true spectrum is not unidimensional; it is multidimensional. It is not linear; it is certainly not as orderly as the DAGMAR communications spectrum would have you believe.
>
> Actually, prospects may enter and leave the communications path at different points. For example, on reaching awareness, prospects may adopt a favorable position, an unfavorable position, or an undecided position. Actually, only those who are undecided are candidates to move forward to the next position— comprehension. The others may have decided for or against any action. Those who decide favorably may skip directly to action. Those who attain an unfavorable position may subconsciously shrug off further communication. [10]

Opinions on the value of various communication and sales measures for evaluating individual advertisements and campaigns were obtained in a survey of research directors in fifty top-billing advertising agencies. [11] Respondents were asked to consider measurement methods in the broader sense, in terms of measuring advertising effects, rather than the more limited terms of testing specific aspects of copy. They were requested to assume ideal conditions (no time or cost limitations, good performance from outside suppliers, etc.) and to make evaluations in the abstract.

Each agency director was asked to rate nine different measuring methods used in copy tests as being of "highest value," "real value," "some value," "rather minor value," or "no value." The results are shown in Figure 4.4.

Using a similar rating system, the research directors then were asked their opinions on some preferred measures for evaluating advertising campaigns. These responses are presented in Figure 4.5.

The results of this study illustrate a rather general consensus as to the value of comprehension, attitude, recall, and behavioral measures for campaign research, and wide support for attitude measures as a criterion for campaign effectiveness.

In itself, however, this consensus does not provide any guarantee of the validity of the measures or any support for the hierarchy

FIGURE 4. 4

Rated Values of Nine Measuring Techniques for
Evaluating Individual Advertisements

Measuring Method	Highest Value or Real Value	Some Value, Minor Value, or No Value	Other	No Answer
Recognition	6	34	0	0
Recall	25	13	1	1
Attitude	25	13	1	1
Comprehension	32	8	0	0
Believability	15	24	0	1
Persuasion	5	34	0	1
Buying Predis- position	21	18	0	1
Ad rating	5	34	0	1
Behavioral	25	13	1	1

FIGURE 4. 5

Rated Values of Five Measuring Techniques
for Evaluating Advertising Campaigns

Measuring Method	Highest Value or Real Value	Some Value or Minor Value	Other	No Answer
Awareness	24	13	2	1
Recognition	6	33	1	0
Recall	16	22	1	1
Attitude	30	9	1	0
Buying predis- position	24	13	1	2

assumption. So, before using any of these techniques, one should examine the evidence concerning the *link* between the measure used and final purchase behavior, or alternatively the *link* between one measure and another, given that the latter is in turn linked to the purchase behavior.

In the following pages, the relationships between verbal response and purchase behavior will be examined. The three major types of verbal response — *awareness, knowledge, and attitude* — will be discussed in turn.

Awareness and Behavior. Most of the proponents of the hierarchy-of-effects theory believe that awareness is, in most cases, a necessary condition for purchase behavior when the measures of awareness are related to the product, brand or company advertised.

In addition to awareness of the subject or object advertised, a number of measurement techniques have been developed to measure the "awareness" of the advertisement itself. The most commonly used of such techniques are the measures of recognition and recall; according to Lucas and Britt, "the memory techniques are outstanding in their popularity as measures of the effectiveness of specific advertisements."[12]

The recognition method, for example, is used in the Starch Advertisement Readership Service. It typically determines from a sample of readers of a particular magazine issue the number who have seen each advertisement, and the number who have read at least half of each advertisement. Summary figures are provided to facilitate comparison with past scores and with the scores of competitors.

The unaided recall method, as another example, is used in the Gallup & Robinson Magazine Impact techniques. It provides more qualitative information than does the recognition method in that recall probes magazine readers' ability to describe advertisements they claim to have seen and to play back the message of the advertiser. Comparable measures are available for the broadcast media, such as in Gallup & Robinson's Total Prime Time Television Surveys. The use of all these methods requires the assumption that the advertisement or claim that is better remembered will lead to more sales.

Large numbers of studies are concerned with the validity of the recognition measures — whether the recognition method overstates or understates the actual "true" number of readers of the advertisement. This question is relevant, however, only if the *link* is established between recognition, recall, or similar measures and sales.

Knowledge and Behavior. Underlying all techniques that measure people's knowledge about a brand, product, or advertisement as indicators of advertising effectiveness is the assumption that the more people know about a brand, a product or advertisement, the more likely they will be to purchase.

This presupposes, however, that all knowledge is positive in nature, so that increases in the amount known will increase the probability of purchase. Yet knowledge has been proved to have both positive and negative effects, depending on the context of its conveyance, the method of its presentation, and its interaction with the recipient's own preconceived ideas and prejudices. Consequently, an increased knowledge can lead to increases, decreases, or no change at all in actual purchase behavior!

Attitude and Behavior. It is commonly agreed that attitude is a construct which must be inferred, rather than an immediately observable or measurable variable.

This being so, attitudes are typically considered as a

predisposition to respond in a particular way toward an object, or event, or a particular set of circumstances. Using this definition, it follows logically that attitudes may have consequence for the way people act (attitudes as determinants of behavior), or at the least can be used to predict future behavior (attitudes as correlates of behavior).

"*Behavioral, attitude* and *opinion* measures, as predictors of future sales behavior, are the *best* measures of the *sales effectiveness* of an individual advertisement. Whether they are actually predictors of sales is a moot point."[13]

To some extent, empirical studies support the assumption of correlation between attitude and behavior. According to Professor Raymond A. Bauer of the Harvard Graduate School of Business Administration: ". . . In the light of more recent writings, it is worth recording that researchers *have* generally found a *discernible, positive* relationship between various measures of attitudes and the overt behavior with which one would assume they would be associated."[14]

In studies such as DeFleur and Westie's experiment on attitudes and overt behavior, there is some evidence supporting a relationship between attitude and behavior.

Verbally expressed, attitudes were significantly related to the direction of the action taken by subjects regarding being photographed with a Negro of the opposite sex.

Are these and similar findings on the relationship between attitudes and overt behavior useful towards demonstrating the validity of attitudinal responses in measuring effectiveness? Such a relationship may merely reflect an individual's established attitudes—toward a brand, for example—as the result of his experience with the brand and not his response to the advertising.

This reasoning has tended to favor a measure of attitude *change* as the desired response. Hence, the question is whether or not an attitude change brought about by exposure to a persuasive communication will lead to changes in subsequent behavior.

There is not much evidence to support *causal* relationship between attitude and behavior. Leon Festinger, psychology professor of Stanford University, has attempted to explore this question: In 1964 he found only three studies which examined the effect of attitude upon behavioral change—in contrast to a single correlation between exisiting attitudes and behavior.

He concluded that there was almost no support for the assumption that attitude change is a necessary and sufficient condition for behavioral change: "What I want to stress is that we have been quietly and placidly ignoring a very vital problem. We have essentially persuaded ourselves that we can simply assume that there is, of course, a relationship between attitude change and subsequent behavior and, since this relationship is obvious, why should we labor to overcome the considerable technical difficulties of investigating it? But the few relevant studies certainly show that this *'obvious' relationship probably does not exist and that, indeed, some nonobvious relationships may exist.''* [16]

This conclusion was supported by DuPont's Malcolm McNiven. Speaking at a National Industrial Conference Board Meeting, he reported on a designed experiment where Medium A caused more attitude change than Medium B, but Medium B caused more sales. [17]

These and other findings imply that causality between attitude and behavior cannot be assumed. Nonetheless, attitudes can be used as correlates (or predictors) of sales. As stated, for example, by Cornelius DuBois: ''. . . The more favorable the attitude among users, the more users you can hold. The more favorable the attitude among nonusers, the more you can bring into the user group. When the attitudes change, behavior follows: moving people up the attitude scale and keeping them there helps your chances of winning them as customers or holding them as customers.'' [18]

The use of attitudes as predictors of sales should be viewed with caution, however. This was clearly indicated from Valentine Appel's experimental findings that if he had depended upon the measured attitudes toward the brand, he would have concluded that the advertising was ineffective. ''The fact is, of course, that the advertising was effective, since it caused a measurable increase in usage.'' [19]

Other empirical findings, especially from the communications literature, touch on the *link* between attitude change and subsequent behavior. The evidence that the use of attitude as the measured response of advertising effectiveness is questionable. It is not clear if a single or even few exposures to advertising can change existing negative attitudes.

In turn, this raises some additional problems concerning the scope of the advertising encompassed by a given measurement technique. Furthermore, the usefulness of attitude measures for established products and brands is highly problematical, considering the difficulty of changing existing attitudes from negative to positive in a test period, and the likelihood of intensifying and reenforcing existing attitudes.

In evaluating advertising for new products, attitude measures theoretically might be more appropriate. Yet the only test of the validity of these measures is their *link* to the ultimate purchase behavior. This implies that an advertising alternative that leads to a higher attitude score also must lead to more purchases than the alternative advertisement.

3. *Internal (Physiological) Responses.* A few agencies and advertisers are experimenting with measures of the physical and

physiological responses of individuals who were exposed to advertisements. Measures of this type are said to be more "objective" than the verbal measures.

The physiological responses, including changes in pulse rates and blood pressure, are of particular interest in that they are not subject to the conscious control of the respondent, who neither reports the responses nor can manipulate them at will. Among the most commonly used physiological responses in advertising measurements are changes in the size and dilation of the pupils of the eyes, in the electrical conductivity of the skin, and in salivation.

Size and Dilation of the Pupils of the Eyes. Measuring changes in pupil size provides an indication of the intensity of response aroused by the viewed design. "When looking at interesting or pleasant materials as compared to neutral ones, the pupil dilates measurably. Conversely looking at distasteful or disliked materials produces contraction." [20]

Herbert E. Krugman, formerly Vice President of Marplan and now a member of the Marketing and Public Relations Research Service of the General Electric Company, suggested a growing conviction, as a result of these studies, that in many areas of human behavior one might make better predictions of behavior from pupil responses than from verbal or opinion data. Reflecting on his research organization's experience with measurement of pupil responses, he concluded that the technique held considerable promise for study of the interest-arousing characteristics of visual stimuli.

"The impact of the environment is often difficult to determine from conscious impressions verbally reported. For a variety of reasons, people may not be practiced or competent to accurately verbalize their feeling in certain areas of living. Pupil measurement seems to provide a powerful new tool for the study of these areas." [21]

Electrical Conductivity of the Skin. Changes in electrical conductivity are induced by the minute degree of perspiration that occurs from exposure to a stimulus. They are measured by a psychogalvanometer attached to the respondent's hand. Audience Studies Incorporated, for example, is using a test of this type.

Salivation. One investigation has considered the use of the unconditioned salivation response as a measure of the effectiveness of appetite appeals. In preliminary tests, increased salivary secretion seemed to occur when a person was shown an appetizing piece of food, after looking at a neutral item.

4. *Physical Responses.* Aside from these physiological responses, some tests have been made in an attempt to measure a person's physical reactions to television commercials by letting him control both the brightness and the sound level. The assumption is that if the subject is interested in the commercial, he will

make more of an effort to sustain the level of brightness and volume than he would for an uninteresting commercial.[22]

A variety of other techniques measures subject's responses, both physical and physiological, to advertising alternatives. There remain two basic problems to be solved, however, before these techniques can become useful measures of advertising effectiveness. The first is the matter of interpretation of results. In commenting on the psychogalvanometer, for example, Lucas and Britt acknowledge the fact that the psychogalvanometer is a completely objective measuring instrument; but they also point out that the question of validity, for advertising research, is another matter.

> Certainly, interpretations of the meaning of galvanic patterns have not become definitive. Extreme fluctuations of the record may indicate excitement, attraction, repulsion, perplexity—or what? Each test subject has a different basic level at the start of every test and, considering the atypical conditions of advertising exposure, it is difficult to know how the galvanic record relates to normal advertising response. [23]*

The second problem in the use of such techniques is that the *links* between these selected physiological responses and subsequent purchase behavior have yet to be substantiated. There is little evidence, unfortunately, concerning the nature of these links.

One of the few reported studies touching this problem concerned the validity of the result of the operant conditioning technique. According to two investigators, data from a controlled experiment indicated that:

> . . . where significant differences are found between commercials in the sales test, significant differences are also found with the operant conditioning technique. Where no significant differences are found, the order of the commercials was the same in the sales test and in the operant conditioning technique. This would indicate that results obtained through the use of operant conditioning could be used to predict the sales-inducing power of commercial messages. [24]

Physical and physiological responses, then, would not seem to be bona fide indicators or predictors of advertising effectiveness, as advertising effectiveness is defined in this book.

---

* [23] From, *Measuring Advertising Effectiveness* by Darrell Blaine Lucas and Steuart Henderson Britt. Copyright 1963 by McGraw-Hill Book Co., Inc. Used with permission.

Purchase and Nonpurchase Measures

Nonpurchase measures of advertising effectiveness include a variety of marketing search activities, physiological and physical responses, and the various verbal responses that are also known as "communication" measures. Some of the *links* among these nonpurchase measures of advertising effectiveness have been discussed in the previous sections.

If one assumes that the final aim in evaluating advertising effectiveness is to relate advertising to sales (and profits), this in turn implies that any meaningful measures of response to advertising alternatives must be related directly or indirectly to sales. On the other hand, some advertisers might advocate nonbehavior measures as sufficient in order to assess the potential effectiveness of advertising alternatives. The differences of opinion among those advocating sales measures and those advocating nonpurchase measures of effectiveness in selecting advertising alternatives stem from varying interpretations of the meaning of effectiveness.

Our own view is that under most circumstances the advertiser who asks, "Which advertising campaign is going to be more effective?" in essence means, "Which advertising campaign is going to be more profitable in the long run?"

Sales or purchase data are used as a measure of effectiveness in both the controlled experiment campaign pretest and in the historical analysis campaign posttests, as explained earlier. In addition, they are sometimes used as the measure of success of a complete campaign by merely comparing sales during the campaign period with sales in the most recent comparable past period. Increases or decreases are presumed to be measures of the campaign's effectiveness or lack of effectiveness.

In general, however, total sales are not considered a valid measure of advertising effectiveness because of the presence of other influencing variables. Sales as a criterion may have some validity if advertising is the most prominent variable, or, in the case of mail order advertising, when it is the only variable.

Many researchers deplore the general acceptance of measures of advertising short of sales or purchases; they frown on communications measures as sole criteria. A statement by Kristian Palda is typical:

> It is notorious that sales measures of advertising effectiveness are employed scantily, and a good case can be made for the claim that the general acceptance of the idea of a hierarchy of advertising effects is to a large extent responsible for this. [25]

Where sales are used as a measure of effectiveness, figures provided by such firms as the A.C. Nielsen Company, Audits and Surveys, and the Market Research Corporation of America may be useful instead of (or along with) a firm's own figures.

In the study of the fifty agency research directors noted

earlier, respondents were asked to give their opinions on methods for evaluating campaigns for their sales effects; and 27 of 37 respondents to the question of whether or not sales effects of campaigns are obtainable replied in the affirmative. Statements by the majority point out:

> . . that sales effects have been measured, that case histories are available, that controlled experiments have continually proven their potential, and that it is merely a question of enough time and money to do accountability studies properly. In other words, it appears that suitable sales data may not be generally available, but that such data can presently be obtained. [26]

The lack of adequate resources for measuring sales effects from advertising was a key point. In the words of one respondent:

> Isolating sales effects of advertising requires more money rather than improved techniques. Given adequate research funds, most (not all) campaigns could be assigned a sales result. [27]

The research directors were divided equally on the question of whether or not sales should be used as the chief campaign criterion. In evaluating advertising campaigns, the values attached to the following four methods of individual advertisement testing were much the same. These differences were noted, however:

> *Attitude measures* become the highest rated criterion for campaign effectiveness.
>
> *Recall measures* receive less than majority support as a highly valuable method.
>
> *Measures of awareness,* not evaluated for individual advertising testing, received a favorable vote of nearly two-to-one for campaign evaluation.
>
> *Measurement of the sales influence of advertising campaigns,* while conceded to be possible by a large majority, reached a deadlock as to desirability for use as a final criterion. [28]

Those individuals preferring sales measures to nonpurchase measures concede that the latter (communications effects, for example) in general are more readily measurable and, for a given expenditure, more reliable. But they do not believe that this necessarily makes them more acceptable.

The critical shortcoming of nonpurchase measures of advertising effectiveness lies in the difficulty, indeed often the impossibility, of establishing a realistic relationship between communications or any other nonpurchase measures and sales measures. Consequently, it is claimed, most advertisers have no objective basis for deciding whether an additional unit of, say, advertisement recall or awareness will produce additional sales or profit dollars.

Advocates of sales as a measure of advertising effects emphasize the value of having advertising results stated in terms that are directly comparable with results of other business functions. Acknowledging the problems involved, Martin Mayer, in the Advertising Research Foundation booklet *The Intelligent Man's Guide to Sales Measures of Advertising,* reflects the cautious hopes of the proponents of sales:

> A decade's work in the direct measurement of the sales effectiveness of advertising has left researchers still groping, trying, failing more often than they succeed. The hurdles that still stand in the way will take a lot of jumping: direct measurement is still difficult, expensive, time-consuming, and disruptive of normal operations. But there are detailed success stories on the record from the U.S. Department of Agriculture and from Du Pont; and at least half a dozen other very large corporations are known to be working along these lines. Given the probable improvement of techniques and the certain improvement of machinery, much more such research seems inevitable in the years ahead. [29]

However, the pros and cons are by no means unambiguous in telling advertising management what to do. As Charles K. Ramond, business professor at Columbia University and editor of the *Journal of Advertising Research,* has remarked ". . . advertising can communicate in ways not all of which necessarily lead to sales. Knowledge of the advertising message is only sometimes a reflector of sales power, and even changed awareness of the brand may not be a necessary condition for an increase in sales." [30]

Those who prefer nonpurchase measures of advertising performance cite the practical difficulties involved in relating advertising results to sales. Some take the position that advertising as a communication tool may successfully carry out its function but that other factors may outweigh or counteract the communication effects in the actual purchase situation. Thus, although the communication effort might be successful, the sale might go elsewhere. Hence, it is impractical to attempt to develop a meaningful relationship between advertising and sales.

Russell Colley disallows sales figures as the final yardstick of advertising performance *unless* the situation is such that:

1. Advertising is the single variable in a controlled experiment, or
2. Advertising is the dominant force in the marketing mix, or
3. The proposition calls for immediate payout (such as in mail order or retail advertising).

He contends that these conditions are generally not found with "nationally advertised products," and goes on to explain the function of advertising thus:

> Advertising does not physically impel the consumer toward the purchase of goods; its purpose is to create a state of mind conducive to purchase. Advertising, therefore, is one of several communication forces which, acting singly or in combination, move the consumer through successive levels of what we have termed the communication spectrum. . . . *The purpose of advertising is to perform certain parts of the communicating job with greater economy, speed and volume than can be accomplished through other means.* [31]

Blaine Cooke, marketing vice president of United Air Lines, takes a somewhat reluctant stand in favor of nonpurchase measures:

> Ever since DAGMAR, it seems, commentators on the subject of advertising research have had to choose up sides, to identify themselves as communicators or salesmen. It is unfortunate that so useful a work as DAGMAR has resulted in so gross an oversimplification. Yet if a choice had to be made, I guess that I would find myself on the side of the so-called communicators. [32]

Perhaps these positions can best be understood in the light of the communications theories of advertising performance—illustrated by the theory of "hierarchy of effects" and its alternative theory of "correlates of effects."

Two factors seem to be operating. The first is the willingness of an advertiser to accept the causal or correlating link between communications and overt purchase behavior hypothesized by these theories. The second is the recognition of the relative ease of implementation and reliability of communications measures compared to sales measures.

The closer a measure is to direct sales results, the less critical becomes the reliance upon any hypothesized links; but in general it also becomes more difficult to implement and offers less reliable results. This "tradeoff" is illustrated in Figure 4.6.

Generally speaking, a measurement technique that is strong in one factor is weak in the other. For example, a technique that measures advertisement recall is relatively easy to implement, but one must assume there is a relationship between recall and purchase behavior. An actual market test, on the other hand, is both expensive and difficult to carry out, but its results are expressed in dollar terms.

Most of the measurement techniques fall somewhere between the two extremes of the continuum. Thus, in choosing a specific technique some tradeoff is necessary between the two aims—ease of implementation, and reliance on the unproven link between the nonpurchase and purchase measures. For a decision that must be made almost immediately, an advertiser may be willing to use a technique that involves rather tenuous assumptions.

FIGURE 4. 6

Nonpurchase and Purchase Measures

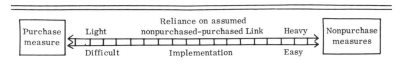

Given more time to carry out a test, and perhaps more money as well, the same advertiser might prefer a technique that eliminates some assumptions of the less acceptable method. In other words, the choice of a technique is clearly related to the conditions under which the decision has to be made, as well as the characteristics of the technique itself.

SOME IMPLICATIONS

From a management point of view, the desirability of relating advertising effects to sales or profits can hardly be debated.

The preceding discussion indicates that there is no conclusive empirical support for the validity of the theoretical concept underlying the "hierarchy-of-effects" assumption; that is, there is *no* conclusive evidence on the causal link between nonpurchase and purchase measures.

On the other hand, there is some empirical evidence, although not conclusive, supporting the assumption of "correlates-of-effects," that is, evidence on the link between various nonpurchase and purchase measures. This evidence seems to provide strong support for the use of tests which incorporate sales results.

The difficulty with these tests, of course, is in overcoming the problems that in many cases accompany them. To avoid these problems, many advertisers undoubtedly will continue to use communications or other nonpurchase measurement techniques. By doing so, they imply a willingness to accept an assumed but empirically unproved relationship between nonpurchase measures and sales. However, for many advertisers this assumption probably is preferable to dealing with the additional problems that would be encountered in carrying out sales tests.

Certain circumstances, however, may warrant using a sales measure in spite of the problems involved—for example, when an advertising decision is particularly important and costly. In certain instances the advertiser may seek to establish a criterion or "bench mark" for judging other advertising results. Additional research then might indicate that within a given product class (as an illustration, a high-volume, packaged food item distributed principally through supermarkets), an X percent increase in brand awareness within a market will generally result in a Y percent increase in sales.

Thus, both sales measures and nonpurchase measures can be useful to advertisers, whose measurement requirements necessarily differ over time. In cases where there is reason to doubt the assumed relationship between nonpurchase results and sales, some type of sales test seems a logical choice, other conditions permitting. But if conditions do not permit, a communication or other nonpurchase test might be chosen.

V

Assumptions Concerning the Environmental Factors

REJECTION OF THE ASSUMPTIONS concerning the context attributes of a measuring technique means that the particular technique should not be used. On the other hand, acceptance of the context assumptions does not rule out the need for continuation of the analysis; a careful examination is still required of the assumptions concerning the attributes of the environmental measurement factors.

FURTHER BASIC ASSUMPTIONS

The assumptions concerning deviations from those five attributes of IMP are presented next.

3. Conditions of Exposure

For an "ideal" measurement technique, or using IMP, the relative effectiveness of advertisements must be measured in the advertising's *natural surroundings,* and the advertisements must be presented in their *natural advertising context.* These ideal conditions of exposure are consistent with the expressed preferences of the research directors of top-billing agencies:

> More than twice as many research directors (21) favored natural conditions of exposure of test copy as favored force exposure (10), while nine made no distinction. [1]

For all post measures, then, and for those pretests of advertising effects involving natural conditions of exposure, no assumptions are required concerning this since actual conditions correspond to the ideal (IMP).

On the other hand, in order to accept a pretest technique that does not present the advertising in its natural context, it must be assumed that the unnatural context will not affect the relative rankings of the advertising alternatives. Can this assumption reasonably be made?

The present authors are not aware of any empirical evidence regarding the effect on respondents' behavior of an artificial, unfamiliar surrounding. It can be assumed, however, that in all nonnatural exposure situations, the respondents tend to behave as a captive audience. In a movie theater, for example, exposure rates are likely to be higher than would obtain under natural conditions. Hence, the following hypothetical situation can be envisioned.

> Advertisements A and B are presented in an artificial pretest environment. Advertisement A has a very strong attention-getting appeal and advertisement B presents a rationale for using a given brand. Under the artificial conditions, both advertisements got actual exposure of close to 100 percent, and advertisement B ranked highest in all the responses measured. In this case it is very likely that the particular attribute of advertisement A—the "attention getting" of those who tend, for example, to leave their TV set whenever a commercial is shown—was not reflected in the pretest. It is conceivable that under actual market conditions advertisement A led to more sales than advertisement B.

A number of studies support the claim that the overall effectiveness of advertising is influenced by the audience characteristics of the vehicle(s) used and by the editorial environment and specific advertising context provided by the vehicle. Hence, if the natural advertising context has some impact on the audience response, a pretest that does not take these factors into account might yield misleading conclusions. The failure to provide the natural editorial context can affect the results of a pretest technique whether the advertising is tested without any media or whether it is tested in a single medium or vehicle when it is actually to be placed in others.

As to differences in the kinds of responses by consumers to different media, the quality of these responses "may occur at a level different from those revealed by audience measurements, or at a considerable lead in time over them." [2]

Regarding the impact of the vehicle, Richard H. Ostheimer, director of research for Time, Inc., has commented that the effectiveness of advertising is influenced by the accompanying editorial material which, in a sense "rubs off" on the advertising. [3]

A number of findings from the field of communication research support this idea of the effect of editorial environment. The effect on audience response of source credibility (the magazine, *True*, versus the newspaper, *The New York Times*, for example) has been studied for some years. Carl I. Hovland, Irving L. Janis, and Harold H. Kelley, in their now classical book, *Communication and Persuasion,* summarized the results of a number of early studies indicating that

1. "Communications attributed to low credibility sources tended to be considered more biased and unfair in presentation than identical ones attributed to high credibility sources."
2. "High credibility sources had a substantially greater immediate effect on the audience's *opinions* than low credibility sources."
3. "The effects on opinion were not the result of differences in the amount of attention or comprehension . . . Variations in source credibility seem to influence primarily the audience's motivation to accept the conclusions advocated."
4. "The positive effect of the high credibility sources and the negative effect of the low credibility sources tended to disappear after a period of several weeks." [4]

Caution is needed in applying communication research findings to advertising, however. One must consider differences in content of the research and its import to the subjects (communication studies generally delving in areas more vital than advertising) and the question of relevance to advertising. Yet despite these qualifications, credibility studies clearly indicate that the "editorial context" of a medium can affect audience response.

A number of communication studies, especially the first of the Yale studies in attitude and communication, *The Order of Presentation in Persuasion,* [5] indicate that under certain conditions the location of the message in the communication process also might affect the audience response. The effect of an advertisement's placement within a vehicle, for example, was studied by Nowland and Company in a 1962 study conducted for *Life* magazine. The study involved testing identical advertisements in different magazines, using an experimental design to rotate the sequence in which the advertisements were presented to respondents. The conclusion as summarized by Richard H. Ostheimer was that,

> . . . the response to advertising is affected by the medium context in which the advertising appears. Clear and significant differences were observed in preferences for identical advertisements when, by the experimental design, the only source of these differences was the medium environment in which the advertisements were exposed. . . [6]

Several additional examples of some recent attempts at measuring the impact of the editorial environment of advertising are:

1. "A Measuring of Advertising Effectiveness—the Influence of Audience Selectivity and Editorial Environment," a study of *McCall's* magazine by Alfred Politz Research, Inc., and involving audience members of *McCall's, Look,* and *Life;*
2. "A Study of the Retention of Advertising in Five Magazines," a study conducted for *This Week* and *Parade* by W.R. Simmons & Associates Research, Inc.;
3. "A Study of Advertising Memorability among Readers of

Life Magazine and Viewers of Prime Time Television Programs," a study conducted by W.R. Simmons & Associates Research, Inc.

In such studies as these, it is assumed that any difference in advertising effectiveness is a result of the editorial climate supplied by each vehicle. That is, if comparable groups of readers are exposed to identical or comparable advertisements in two vehicles, the difference in effectiveness is due to the setting which each vehicle creates.

These and other relevant studies tend to support the contention that nonnatural conditions of exposure will affect the audience response. There is no reason to believe otherwise until some evidence is presented that an advertisement ranking highest in nonnatural conditions of exposure also ranks highest under natural market conditions.

4. Conditions of Measurement

Most of the current methods for obtaining data on audience response to advertising and the measurement environments of the various techniques differ considerably from the ideal conditions represented by IMP.

Consequently, in accepting any of these measurement techniques, certain assumptions must be made, implicitly or explicitly, concerning the conditions of measurement. First, if the method of data collection is other than direct observation of response or if it is carried out with the respondents' knowledge, it must be assumed that this will not affect the results to the extent that rankings of the advertising alternatives will be altered. Second, if the measurement environment is artificial, it must be assumed that this will not have any significant effect on the results, that is, an effect that might change the rankings of the advertising alternatives.

There do not appear to be any empirical studies that test and verify these assumptions directly. Yet, there are numerous pieces of evidence to indicate that both the method of data collection and the measurement environment can lead to deviation from the "true, uncontaminated, natural" response.

The severity of the biases introduced by the method of data collection cannot be separated operationally for the purpose of validating the relevant assumption from the response measured. The verbal (communication) measures are subject to the most severe possible biases of both the interviewer and interviewee. The observed physiological and behavioral measures, when the latter are not reported by the subjects, are presumably subject only to interviewer or observer bias.

There are various elements of bias that either interviewer or observer can introduce. Systematic differences from interviewer to interviewer or systematic errors on the part of any or all interviewers may create significant deviations in the questioning of subjects and the eliciting and recording of responses. Even when the direct data collection is accomplished by a machine—the psychogalvanometer, for example—still there is room for bias in the recording and the interpretation of results.

Personal biases, the interviewer's own preconceptions or expectations or ideas, may cause him to see what he *expects* to see rather than what is there. Some of the more obvious types of interviewer bias can be avoided through appropriate methods of selection and training and standardized interview procedures, yet some is likely to remain.

Similarly, interviewee bias is likely to be expected when a verbal response is solicited from the subject. A problem in using communication measures is that they not only measure awareness, attitude, and the like, but that they also can engender favorable or unfavorable attitudes, "acceptable" and "rationalized" responses. Conscious or unconscious biases on the part of the interviewee may develop during the course of the interviews in the form of defense mechanisms, ego involvement, prestige identification, faulty memory, etc.

While interviewer and interviewee bias primarily results from the method of data collection, it is dependent to a large extent on the specific content of the study. That is, the degree of bias introduced into the study might depend on the particular product, or brand, or advertising elements. It can be assumed, for example, that the use of a highly suggestive theme in a commercial would introduce far more bias into the measurement results than would less sensitive or controversial advertising elements.

The measurement environment—the testing environment in general, and the specific measurement situation—can also contribute to interviewee bias. In view of many findings from the behavioral sciences, it seems plausible to assume that people behave differently under test situations from the way they would under normal nontest conditions. Hence, a measurement technique that de-emphasizes the "test" condition is likely to cause less bias. Using a movie theater for testing TV commercials, for example, constitutes an artificial environment, yet it represents a far less severe test atmosphere than does a laboratory for measuring physiological response.

The specific measurement situation also can contribute to the interviewee's bias, for example, through a fatigue effect, inconvenient timing of the measurement, etc. The contribution of various conditions of measurement to interviewer and interviewee bias has been discussed previously. It is not known, of course, to what extent the bias which results from a condition of measurement deviant from the Idealized Measurement Procedure will affect an available measurement technique. It seems reasonable to assume that the smaller the bias, the greater the probability that the rankings of the advertising alternatives in the pretest and the real world will be positively correlated.

5. Sampling Procedure

For one to have confidence in an advertising measurement technique, it must be assumed that the sampling of people or families or units involved in the measurement will rank the alternatives in essentially the same order as would a very large, unrestricted probability sample of individuals or families or units drawn from the entire relevant population.

It should be emphasized that it is the sample's *responses* which must be representative and not necessarily the sample itself. Nevertheless, a reasonable assumption is that the more representative the composition of the sample, the more representative will be its response.

The sample element used in IMP is an individual. Yet to use any of the other sample elements, such as families, retail outlets, or geographic areas, little is required in the way of assumptions if the sample is chosen properly. The purchases associated with any of these units, with proper handling, could reflect accurately the effectiveness of the advertising.

Restrictions in the sample bring numerous possible sources of error. Should response to the advertising be related to the basis of the restriction, serious misrankings may occur. For example, certain advertising measurement services select their sample from inhabitants of particular metropolitan areas; consequently, usage patterns peculiar to these areas may cause sample responses to be different from average responses throughout the nation. Or an anti-freeze manufacturer may use a pretesting technique which happens to draw its sample from Los Angeles, or New York, or Dallas. In any of these situations, the sample respondents *may* order the advertising alternatives exactly as they would be by a nationwide representative sample; yet advertisers, lacking proof, would have to assume the sufficiently representative native of the sample in order to use that technique.

A similar assumption would have to be made if advertising to be placed in *Life* magazine were tested in the *Saturday Evening Post*. If the specific media vehicle of the test is different from the one in which the advertising is to be placed ultimately, one must assume that the test audience is sufficiently similar to the actual audience that its responses will result in a like ranking of alternatives.

A frequently serious restriction is that of nonparticipation. If a large proportion of those selected for the sample either can't be reached or refuse to participate, the representativeness of those who do participate is open to question. In order to rely on the results of the measurement, one must assume that the nonparticipants would yield responses essentially similar to those of the actual participants. Or one can go on to interview a representative sample of both participant and nonparticipant groups for confirmation of results.

In applying IMP, the probability that each member of the relevant population will appear in the sample is known in advance. Some techniques use probability methods to choose participants within the constraints of their geographic and/or media restrictions. The advantage of using probability sampling is that the existing body of sampling theory can be used to estimate the reliability of the results.

However, high costs and high rates of nonparticipation often associated with probability samples sometimes make nonprobability samples seem more attractive. Representativeness of the sample is a problem here, since the method by which the sample is chosen can introduce biases into the results. But properly handled, nonprobability sampling may prove quite satisfactory in actually being representative of the population under study. Only judgment, not statistical sampling theory, is available to support this statement.

Finally, the sample sizes used vary appreciably in different measurement techniques. Yet, as mentioned earlier, sample size alone is not a measure of the reliability of a measurement technique. Rather, the adequacy of a particular sample depends on the sensitivity of its response to advertising. The more sensitive the response is to advertising, the smaller the sample that is required in order to detect differences in the various advertising alternatives. In general, those responses which are most directly relevant to sales (for example, purchase) tend to be less sensitive to advertising than responses more ambiguous in nature (for example, noting, liking, recall, etc.).

Hence, for an advertiser to have confidence in the results of a particular advertising measurement technique he must assume that the responses of the sample upon which measurement results are based are actually representative of the responses of the population or audience toward which he will direct his advertising. In addition, he must be assured that the sample size and sampling procedures are such that the resulting measurements will be sufficiently reliable as to produce consistent results.

6. Type of Comparison

The Idealized Measurement Procedure (IMP) provided for a simultaneous direct comparison of advertising alternatives in order to devise their relative effectiveness. While some techniques, such as the Marder Ad Evaluation Program and split runs, do provide for a direct simultaneous comparison of alternatives, others deviate in various ways.

Many techniques, including most pretests, can compare

alternatives by measuring them at different times. When the technique is used in this way, it is necessary to assume that events occuring between measures, such as competitive advertising, do not have a substantial influence on the ranking of the alternatives. The longer the time lag between the measurement of the alternatives, the more difficult and serious this assumption becomes.

Some techniques, including both pretests (such as the Schwerin Standard TV Testing Service) and post measures (such as the Starch Readership Service) provide "norms" against which to compare the performance of a particular advertising alternative. In general, the assumption associated with the use of a norm is that, should a large number of independent alternatives be generated and tested, their average would constitute the norm; hence, comparison with a norm is equivalent to comparing an alternative with the average score of the other alternatives. This assumption is perfectly compatible with the ideal of direct comparison with alternatives.

The acceptability of this assumption depends on the way in which the norm is derived. If the norm reflects the average score of previous advertising in a single medium for the particular brand whose advertising later is being tested in the same medium, it must be assumed that intervening events such as a change in the brand's market position, have not affected appreciably the current average advertising performance for the brand. If the media vehicles from which the norm is derived are not precisely the same media vehicles in which advertising performance is measured, these differences also must be either accounted for or assumed away. If the norm includes the former advertising performance of other brands as well, it must be assumed that the previous advertising performance of these other brands, on the average, is the same as the average current advertising possibilities of the brand under study.

In the measurement of advertising effectiveness after the fact, performance is sometimes measured against a "goal," although the concept of what the goal represents, unfortunately, is not always clear. In some cases the goal is interpreted as the forecast level of attainment of an "average" advertising alternative. Another interpretation is that it is the forecast level of attainment of an outstanding advertising alternative (for example, among the top ten percent of all alternatives that might have been used). Either of these two interpretations are consistent with the notion of relative effectiveness.

Clearly, the acceptability of the assumption of what represents a "good" measure of the advertisement reflects how the goal was derived. If the goal is a measure reflecting the historical performance of other campaigns, it is similar to a norm except that it usually is not so well documented. Still, all the assumptions associated with the use of a norm apply.

A third interpretation of the "goal" is that it is the "task" of advertising derived from marketing considerations. As such, the goal (as a standard against which to compare the performance of advertising) is inconsistent with the notion of relative effectiveness. Should the results fall short of the goal, it is impossible to determine whether it was an outstanding campaign nevertheless and the goal was unrealistic, or whether it was simply an inferior campaign.

Techniques in which an advertising alternative is compared with a control—the absence of the advertising in question—are inconsistent with the notion of relative advertising effectiveness unless the possibility of not advertising is a practicable alternative. Hence, unless norms are available or other alternatives are tested as well, the results of such a technique are not interpretable in this framework.

7. Data Handling

In the Idealized Measurement Procedure, the data on observed purchases associated with each alternative would be translated into differences in contributions to profits via the use of estimated incremental profits and advertising costs in each period. The differences in contributions to profits would be discounted to a present value to determine the relative effectiveness of the alternatives. No mechanical or human errors would occur in the data handling process.

Unfortunately, the ideal of faultless data handling is rarely obtained in practice. To accept the results of a measurement process, one must assume that any errors that may have occurred during data handling were not of a magnitude to change the ranking of the alternatives from what they would have been without the errors. This assumption is perhaps most crucial when the responses obtained are subject to interpretation before being tabulated, as in open-ended questions. Such questions are particularly vulnerable to errors causing misranking.

Another deviation from the ideal that occurs in some techniques is the differential weighting of some participants' responses. Frequently this is done to rectify demographic imbalances in the sample. Unfortunately, it leads to effective sample sizes smaller than actual sample sizes, which in turn result in less statistical reliability.

SOME IMPLICATIONS

The last two chapters have dealt with the assumptions that advertising practitioners must make, in selecting and utilizing any current technique for measuring advertising effectiveness. As was indicated previously, certain assumptions are needed in order to bridge the gap between the seven attributes of a given technique and the seven ideal attributes of the Idealized Measurement Procedure (IMP).

It has been emphasized that the use of a measuring technique for assessing the relative effectiveness of two or more equal cost advertising alternatives requires the following assumption: the advertising alternative accorded highest rank when assessed by a given measurement technique would be likely also to rank highest if measured by IMP. The overall assumption, applicable to all seven attributes of IMP, requires rank correlation only, rather than the straight statistical correlations of available test scores against scores obtained by an idealized standard.

Comparing the seven attributes or basic elements of any technique with Idealized Measurement Procedure aids the advertiser in reducing the hazards of accepting a faulty or misleading technique. It helps to specify the assumptions underlying any available technique by reducing the process to seven elemental attributes, about which specific new assumptions can be made for each.

The seven attributes of IMP, as well as the assumptions which must be made in comparison of techniques with IMP, were designed to be independent entities. However, there are some interactions among them. For example, the conditions of measurement closely interact with the type of response measured. This interaction is illustrated by the fact that psychological measurements almost always are associated with a laboratory situation.

In evaluating a technique for measuring advertising effectiveness, all of the assumptions underlying the seven attributes should be considered as an integrated whole, taking into account the relative importance of each assumption. This primarily subjective, yet systematic, procedure will assess all the relevant circumstances— the product advertised, nature of the advertising, time and cost constraints, previous experience with the various measurement techniques, etc. The specific managerial utilization of this analysis is discussed in the following chapter.

VI

Applications of IMP in Analyzing Measurement Techniques

CLEARLY, IF AN IDEALIZED Measurement Procedure (IMP) were completely practicable, it could provide an ideal operational measure of what is known as relative advertising effectiveness.

Although impossible to attain, an ideal standard of comparison does provide a practical framework for comparing and selecting the best suited available measurement technique for any given situation. The selected technique can then test alternative advertising and, subject to stated limitations and assumptions, will yield the desired evaluations of these alternatives.

Realistically, factors other than validity must be evaluated in selecting a measurement technique. Usually the most valid technique or service is assumed to be the one which requires the user to make the fewest compromises and/or least vital assumptions compared to the idealized measurement procedure. Costs and timing also constitute important considerations. The former encompasses not only the obvious out-of-pocket costs but associated manpower and time costs as well, and occasional penalties incurred by the disruption of normal operations. To select an appropriate technique the research manager must estimate whether techniques that are more expensive, but which he considers more reliable, are worth the additional cost. Time factors associated with different techniques also can act as constraints on their use. For example, techniques require long lead times, eliminating them from consideration in some situations.

The present chapter includes a discussion about reconciling the various factors and assumptions associated with particular measurement techniques, so as to enable the selection of the most appropriate technique for the task at hand. The validation of measurement techniques also is discussed, and a more feasible "secondary" standard of comparisons is proposed.

By analyzing the techniques discussed in this chapter, one can decide more objectively which of the techniques is most likely to yield valid results for a particular measurement problem.

In comparing techniques, a subjective evaluation of the necessary assumptions, their relative importance, and their possible effects should indicate the technique that offers the most attractive combination of assumptions, the second most attractive, third, etc. This evaluation process ranks the advertising measurement techniques with respect to their assumed validity.

ADVERTISING MEASUREMENT FOR ADVERTISING MANAGEMENT

Stated as a formal procedure, there are some six steps to follow in utilizing IMP as a guide for advertising decision making or evaluation of alternatives:

1. Assemble a list of the techniques feasible to use in the particular situation. A technique is feasible if a) its results will be ready in time for the conclusions to be put to use, b) the costs are not totally unacceptable, c) it is applicable to the relevant advertising alternatives being measured, and d) there are no "political" barriers to its use.
2. Using the comparative analysis procedure discussed in this book, explicitly state the assumptions required to make each technique acceptable.
3. Examine the assumptions associated with each technique and assemble the available evidence and/or accepted principles which relate to the acceptability of the assumptions.
4. Eliminate all techniques requiring any assumption that is totally unacceptable.
5. Of the remaining techniques, determine via subjective judgment, based on available evidence, the technique that has the most acceptable assumptions in terms of their importance and their deviation from the Idealized Measurement Procedure.
6. Continue ranking the techniques according to the relative acceptability of their assumptions.

The end result of this process will be a list of feasible techniques ranked in order of their assumed validity. Figure 6.1 illustrates such a list.

The fact that technique B in the following example has the most acceptable assumptions does not imply, however, that it is the technique to be selected. The *cost* of each technique must be considered as well. Hence, an estimate of the total costs of the relevant techniques should be undertaken.

As suggested earlier, the cost of a technique is composed of two major elements. First, there are the direct costs either of purchasing the use of a syndicated service or of conducting a study that utilizes the particular measurement technique. Second, indirect costs such as time and inconvenience, while not expressed originally in dollars, must be included in the final analysis. After estimating the direct and indirect costs one then combines the acceptability ranks with the costs of the techniques.

To illustrate the procedure, Figure 6.2 is an example of the hypothetical ranking in order of acceptability from Figure 6.1, and sets a hypothetical cost for each technique.

In this example, technique C is easily eliminated from further consideration. More expensive than either technique F or B, its assumptions are also less acceptable for this application. The remaining techniques are listed in descending order of both cost and acceptability of assumptions.

Intuition and experience can be marshalled at this point to assess the expected dollar value associated with the increasing acceptability of each higher ranking method in comparison to cost. If the greater acceptability of technique B's assumptions is judged to be worth $1,000 more than technique F, the latter is rejected. The same type of comparison then is made between technique B and A, and so on down the list. Each time technique B is considered worth the increment in cost, the other technique is rejected and the comparison continued, one pair at a time.

At some point in the comparisons a lower-ranked method

FIGURE 6.1

A Hypothetical Ranking of Feasible Measurement
Techniques in Order of Their Assumed Validity

Technique	Rank
B	1
F	2
C	3
A	4
D	5
E	6

FIGURE 6.2

Acceptability Rank and Costs of Measurement Techniques

Methods Ranked by Decreasing Acceptability of Assumptions (from Figure 6.1)	Cost of Each Technique
B	$6,000
F	5,000
C	7,500
A	3,000
D	2,500
E	800

may represent a sufficiently large cost saving to warrant the lower level of acceptability. For example, technique A is less acceptable than techniques B or F, but it also costs less. If the cost difference is enough to warrant using the technique despite the lower acceptability of its assumptions, then A would replace B as the first choice.

In a similar manner, technique A then would be compared with each technique ranked below it. Technique D, which is only $500 cheaper than A, may not offer a sufficient cost difference to be attractive. Technique E, however, is considerably less expensive than A, and may be worth using in spite of its less acceptable assumptions. At the end of this process, one method emerges as being overall the most efficient for the purpose at hand.

Comparing techniques in this manner should result in the selection of the technique most appropriate to a particular measurement problem. An even more important result could be the development of new techniques, the characteristics of which might lessen the severity of the assumptions required for specific products or situations. The analysis should point to the particular aspects of existing techniques or services which make them especially useful or questionable in any particular situation.

VALIDATING THE MEASUREMENT TECHNIQUES

At the present time, the choice of techniques depends heavily on one's judgment and experience. The method of selection described above presents a systematic framework within which to apply this judgment more effectively. Yet, to improve the method of choosing techniques, or possibly the techniques themselves, it is desirable to be able to validate them.

The measurement of advertising effectiveness involves some further problems. The relative effectiveness of two advertising alternatives depends on the competitive and economic environment in which the alternatives are measured, as well as on the inherent qualities of the alternatives.

Furthermore, any idealized comparison refers to the relative effectiveness of available alternatives at a given time. This is comparable to a snapshot of something which is constantly changing; if the snapshot were taken at a different time, or under different conditions, the object photographed would probably exhibit different characteristics.

In measuring relative advertising effectiveness, we generally must assume that change is slow enough that the alternatives do not reverse their ranking in effectiveness during a brief time period. If this cannot be assumed, or if the specific environmental influences on effectiveness are not known, there is little chance of finding a valid pretesting technique until additional theory or experimentation becomes available to explain the causes of the changes in effectiveness.

The problems encountered in generalizing from the results of previous experience should not be minimized, however. Seldom if ever is one advertising situation exactly like a previous one. The significance of these changes over time remains an issue to be resolved by judgment rather than by objective evidence.

Moreover, a measurement technique may prove to be valid for one class of products and not for another, or for a leading brand but not a minor brand. As an illustration, a measurement technique may be very appropriate for inexpensive, widely distributed products but completely inadequate for costly, rarely purchased items. Hence, a demonstration of the validity of a measurement technique for a limited number of products over a limited period of time cannot necessarily be generalized. Validation involves a lengthy process of review covering a wide range of products, situations, and types of campaigns.

Ideally, one would prefer to have measurement techniques validated against the "true advertising effectiveness" defined in this report as the ideal standard of comparison. Hence, if it were feasible to implement the standard of comparison, it could be used for validation by comparing the output of a given technique with the output of the standard of comparison. For example, one might measure the effectiveness of a large number of advertising campaigns with the ideal standard of comparison and with the measurement techniques being considered. The results would permit a comparison of the "scores" or even the ranking of the campaigns by the standard and the techniques. With such data and a model which indicated the value of increased validity, more objective decisions on the choice of techniques could be made.

Since there exists no fully implemental ideal standard of comparison for advertising effectiveness, validation against such a standard is not possible. At best, one might attempt to validate the various measurement techniques against an actual technique which comes as close as possible to the Idealized Measurement Procedure. Such "near ideal" techniques will be called secondary standards. The secondary standards would be used primarily for validating other techniques, perhaps never as routine measurement tools in their own right. For this reason it is possible to design a measure which is more elaborate, more carefully controlled, and more expensive than could be considered for routine use.

The secondary standard should have two principal properties. First, it should involve the use of purchases or sales as its criterion, since the principal difference between the ideal and most empirical techniques is the use of purchases in the former. Second, its design should be such that at least two and possibly more alternatives could be measured simultaneously; this is necessary, obviously, since the effectiveness is defined in a relative sense.

The form of the secondary standard might vary with different applications. It may be a function of the particular market or product in question. A form which is appropriate for the measurement of automobile advertising effeceveness, for example, might not be appropriate for measuring the effectiveness of detergents or machine tool advertising.

As discussed earlier, there is one method which seems to have the broadest applicability. It is the market test or sales experiment which comes closest to the IMP standard of comparison.

While the details of market tests may vary from one application to another, they consist essentially of exposing a number of populations, often in separate geographic areas, to one of each of the alternatives to be evaluated. The sales response to each alternative is then measured via store audits, pantry checks, or any other appropriate means of data collection.

Controlled Market Experiments

Controlled experiments offer an approach to pretesting the relative effectiveness of two or more alternative advertising campaigns. Frequently, sales response is the criterion used. In controlled market experiments, variables are arranged and controlled so that the influence of each is measured in terms of its apparent impact on sales. The use of sophisticated experimental designs in marketing research is relatively new. That is, there have been few controlled experiments in which adequate statistical sampling methods have been used to measure the effect of changes in one variable (such as sales) in response to changes in one or more variables so as to provide statistical confidence limits on the overall value of the data.

William S. Hoofnagle, chief of the market development branch of the United States Department of Agriculture, has pointed out the virtues of controlled experiments in advertising research:

> A measurement tool being utilized with increasing frequency in examining the effectiveness of different facets of promotion and advertising is the experimental design—a specific plan for research having certain statistical and logical qualities. . . . In most problems where the experimental design is considered as a measurement tool, the researcher is basically interested in a comparison of the relative efficiency of alternatives. . . . Through the chosen design, a measurement is taken of the sales efficiency of the alternatives tested in such a fashion that nothing in the experiment itself favors one alternative over another . . . the Latin square design and variations, along with factorial designs, are the ones that have been adapted most readily to problem solving in the field of promotion and advertising. [1]

The market development branch of the United States Department of Agriculture has used experimental designs in a number of its studies on the effects of agricultural commodity promotion.

One of these studies was carried out in cooperation with the Washington State Apple Commission. It was to determine, among other things, the relative sales effectiveness of two promotional themes:

1. An "apple use" advertising and promotional theme.
2. A general health advertising and promotional theme.

These two "treatments," along with a treatment of no advertising or promotion for control purposes, were tested in six cities during four time periods. Analysis of results showed:

> There were substantial differences in sales of both Washington State and all apples between periods with promotional themes (apple use and health) and periods of no promotion. When sales of apples [Washington State and others] were combined, the apple use theme was significantly more effective in promoting sales than the health theme. However, the nine percent sales difference between the two themes [when limited to] Washington State apples was not large enough to be statistically significant. [2]

Hoofnagle suggests that:

> Success or failure of an experiment depends to a large extent on the depth of planning a project. The researchers should be thoroughly familiar with the commodity or product, the objective of the experimentation, conditions under which the tests are to be conducted, alternative techniques for analysis and interpretation of the data, and use and application of the findings. [3]

Well-conducted, controlled experiments of advertising campaigns, using sales as the measurement criterion, seem closest to the ideal approach. Their relatively limited use to reveal the influence of advertising alone as an independent variable is probably due largely to cost and time factors. Charles K. Ramond, business professor at Columbia University and editor of the *Journal of Advertising Research,* says,

> To determine the contribution of any marketing force to either sales or communication, the experimental method is most likely to provide an unambiguous result, because it eliminates most of the inevitable alternative explanations of naturally observed relationships . . . By now it should be clear that there are no easy ways to evaluate the profitability of advertising and marketing expenditures. The state of the art is sound, but the art itself is costly and complex. Experimentation is recommended, not because it is a panacea, but because in many cases it is the only way to get whatever unambiguous measures may be possible. [4]

However, Edward S. Hughes, survey research department manager at Ford Motor Co., pointed out some of the problems in using experimental designs for measuring effectiveness:

A number of conceptual objections exist with respect to these tests. One concern is that advertising impressions may interact with one another beyond the ability of experimental design to sort them out successfully. Another concern is that sales effectiveness tests may unduly direct management attention toward advertising which produces quick sales at the expense of other possible objectives of the communications process. Operational difficulties probably represent a more valid limitation of this technique. For example, there can be great difficulty in holding the conditions of the experiment constant, and in obtaining reliable sales data for consumers in the various test groups, for a long enough period of time to isolate true sales gains from a temporary acceleration of purchase. Other operational problems can arise from the development and handling of the large samples sometimes required in sales effectiveness tests. These large samples are needed when small percentage gains in sales will result in a profit from an advertising expenditure. [5]

Yet, despite these limitations, a controlled market experiment seems to provide the closest practical approach to an Idealized Measurement Procedure. But, since even the market test deviates from the IMP standard of comparison, it is appropriate to examine the ways in which it deviates and to examine the assumptions required for its use.

Evaluating a Test Market Procedure

The nature of broadcast and print media makes it difficult to control advertising inputs to individuals without their knowledge, as would be done in the ideal test situation. Generally, the closest one can come is to concentrate the advertising inputs into particular communities, which is what the market test does.

This means, however, that the people to be exposed to a given advertising alternative cannot be a probability sample of the entire population. At best, they can be drawn only from the communities exposed to that alternative. Hence, a crucial assumption is that the communities' patterns of media exposure and patterns of response to advertising correspond roughly to the circumstances which would prevail if the entire relevant population (or a well-chosen probablilty sample of it) were exposed to the alternative.

A second deviation of the market test from the ideal test situation is in the actual response measured. The ideal would record individual purchase behavior, while the market test frequently uses audits or other gross means of assessing sales. One must assume that whatever response is measured is closely related to the purchase measure used in the ideal.

A third deviation lies in the method of data treatment. In the ideal situation the contributions to profits generated by people exposed to one alternative versus another alternative simply would be compared. This is possible because the random sampling procedure and the sample size have assured the user that the common population base from which each alternative sample is drawn yields test results which are representative of the population as a whole for all the alternatives tested. In practice, no such assurance usually exists for comparing market test results. Each community (or set of communities) may start from a different base of purchase patterns, market share, and total sales. Unless a very well-chosen and large number of communities are used for each alternative, the analysis probably will require an adjustment or some other normalization of sales to make the results comparable.

Despite these limitations, the market test seems to be the most appropriate applied standard of comparison for field tests and validation. To use this or any other technique as a feasible secondary standard for validation purposes, one has to assume, as a minimum, that the secondary standard on the average will rank a number of campaigns in the same way as IMP would rank them if it could be applied.

However, since this secondary or proxy standard is subject to variations, results might differ from the ideal for any particular ranking. This means that if a set of alternatives were measured twice with the same secondary standard, the subsequent rankings might not agree. The secondary standard ratings would have some rank correlation between the two sets of ranks—and this might be less than perfect (+ 1). Clearly, no technique could hope to correlate with IMP any better than it correlates with itself over a large number of trials.

SOME IMPLICATIONS

This chapter has demonstrated a means by which the Idealized Measurement Procedure can be used as a standard of comparison to choose the best advertising measurement technique for a particular decision situation.

In addition, an approach to validation of measurement techniques has been discussed. For validation purposes, it was proposed that the market test be used as a secondary or proxy standard for actual fieldwork comparisons, since it comes closest to providing an Idealized Measurement Procedure.

VII

Some Conclusions

THE MAJOR POINTS brought out in this book fall into three interdependent areas:

1. Information for advertising decisions
2. Evaluating alternative advertising measurement techniques
3. The meaning of advertising effectiveness

INFORMATION FOR ADVERTISING DECISIONS

For the purpose of making advertising decisions, it is necessary to conceive only of *relative* effectiveness among the advertising alternatives, particularly if they are of relatively equal cost. The notion of *absolute* effectiveness, meaning the "contribution" in some value sense (units or dollars) of advertising to overall marketing effectiveness, requires a much better understanding than is now available of the interactions of factors affecting the marketing process.

The decision criterion that seems most universally preferable is the *present value of relative contributions* to profits. This can be deduced directly from information on relative changes in purchase behavior and a knowledge of associated costs and prices.

Advertising researchers usually use communications measures of advertising performance as a criterion. They base the use of this criterion on the theory of a "hierarchy-of-effects." This theory states, essentially, that people tend to go through measurable attitudinal stages of increasing awareness through commitment to purchase. Bringing a person to successively higher stages is assumed to increase his likelihood of eventual purchase. Since some recent studies tend to discredit this theory, the basis for using only communications measures (such as awareness or recall) to assess the effects of advertising is threatened.

The present study involves an alternative, the assumption of so-called *correlates-of-effects.* This approach emphasizes the use of communications measures only for decision making among equal cost advertising alternatives. For such decisions, it is merely required that the measure result in ranking the alternatives roughly in the same order as they would be ranked if their true relative contributions to sales revenues could be known. It is *not* necessary to know the exact relationship between attitude and purchase, for example, nor to assume that the two are causally related, as in the theory of a hierarchy-of-effects.

For example, if one were to measure attitude and if the true criterion of purchases was reasonably highly correlated with an attitudinal measure, then this correlation would be sufficient justification of the use of attitudes as a good proxy or surrogate for the ideal sales measure.

However, for unequal cost advertising decisions, more information is required. Simply ranking the alternatives is not enough. It is necessary to know, or to assume, a strong relationship between the measures and the relative contributions to revenues of the alternatives.

EVALUATING ALTERNATIVE ADVERTISING MEASUREMENT TECHNIQUES

The Idealized Measurement Procedure (IMP) is introduced as an analytic guide. It gives a target to shoot at in terms of theoretical ideal; and provides a tool for identifying the assumptions embodied in the various available techniques for measuring advertising effectiveness. Once these assumptions are identified, the advertiser can examine the evidence concerning them. He then can evaluate the acceptability of the various techniques for measuring advertising effectiveness based on the evidence, the importance of the assumptions, and his own experience. Given the comparative acceptability rating, the total cost of the various measurement techniques, and the relevant constraints on their utilization, an advertiser has a sound basis for selecting a measurement technique. Further, once a technique has been adopted, its observed deviations from the ideal can provide the advertiser with some feeling concerning the extent to which he may reasonably depend on its results.

Users of the Idealized Measurement Procedure may find it desirable to add or delete various attributes or change the identity of the ideal standard of each attribute. For example, some users may prefer an attitudinal measure as the idealized response. In this case all they have to do is substitute an attitudinal measure for the sales measure proposed earlier and then assess the deviation of feasible techniques from the new ideal basis. The adaptability of the IMP framework reflects the basic flexibility of the proposed analytical procedure.

The evaluative approach outlined provides a guide for the selection and evaluation of assumptions underlying various available techniques, and leaves it to the advertiser's judgment to weight each assumption and the severity of any deviations from the ideal. IMP's flexibility thereby enables broad application and suggests increasingly high payoff to users through their more systematic assessment of alternatives, and their more efficient recording and learning from experience over time.

THE MEANING OF "ADVERTISING EFFECTIVENESS"

The systematic framework of analysis outlined in the foldout exhibit in Chapter III not only serves as a tool for selecting and evaluating advertising measurement techniques but also can help advertising people focus on what they mean specifically by the term "advertising effectiveness." An operational meaning of the term (i.e., a workable and practical concept), far surpassing the traditional notions of advertising effectiveness, is that property of an advertisement or a campaign in which increases are always desirable for the advertiser.

Viewing IMP's seven attributes as a whole, one might think of them as comprising a hypothetical ideal measurement technique or as representing an "idealized operational definition" of relative advertising effectiveness. It is clear, in other words, that while the total attributes and operations of IMP can be conceptualized, they cannot be realized in practice, due to limitations in the technology of marketing science.

Using the IMP analysis as a guideline for evaluating performance and as representing the real meaning of "advertising effectiveness" implies the acceptance of the need for a measure of "relative advertising effectiveness." Such acceptance also implies that *the criterion of relative effectiveness is the difference in the discounted present value (usually in dollars) of the contribution to profit, resulting from the difference in final buyer purchases generated by the sample of buyers exposed to one campaign versus the sample exposed to another.*

The crucial aspect of overall relative advertising effectiveness is assumed to be the difference engendered in the final buyers' purchasing patterns of the advertised product under current conditions of availability and competitive pressure. Both industrial buyers and household consumers are considered to be "final" buyers.

All other possible effects of the advertising on relative profitability are ignored. Conceptually, the relative effectiveness notion implies the difference between what would happen if one campaign were run "normally" versus what would happen if another campaign were run normally. One can imagine observing the results of the first campaign, then stopping the world and backing up to the point of decision, inserting the alternative campaign, and observing its results, then contrasting the two.

The impossibility of such a procedure is obvious. By contrast the proposed IMP approach to analysis is conceptually feasible and provides some initial steps toward a better understanding of the meaning of advertising effectiveness.

FINAL CONSIDERATIONS

The present book presents a new operational approach to the evaluation of techniques for measuring advertising effectiveness. At the same time it indicates directions for future research on advertising effectiveness.

More specifically, it suggests directing research efforts toward the assumptions linking the attributes of the various measurement techniques and the attributes of the primary standard IMP and any secondary standards such as test market procedures. Because so little is known today about these relationships, such studies might be of substantial value in shedding light on the validity of the various techniques for measuring advertising effectiveness. This validation could serve as the key to the development of more comprehensive and testable theory of advertising.

At present, IMP represents perfection and, as such, is not directly implementable. However, secondary standards, such as market tests, can be used after they have been compared with the Idealized Measurement Procedure.

As an ideal, the IMP comparative analysis framework can be used in connection with many different kinds of advertising, as well as for many different measurement techniques. It is applicable to industrial as well as product or service advertising. It is relevant for any technique having the same basic attributes as the stated ideal. In practice, this includes all the more popular techniques (many of which are compared with IMP in Chapter III) and numerous others which are not specifically mentioned.

This methodology, representing a standard against which available measurement techniques can be compared, expresses the authors' convictions as to what should be meant by "advertising effectiveness." Hopefully, this approach will stimulate others to undertake additional theoretical and empirical work in this area. With the development of theoretically sound and empirically supported guidelines, advertising decision making and evaluation of techniques for measuring advertising effectiveness can be put on a more objective, sound, and reasonable basis.

Footnotes

CHAPTER I.   MEASUREMENT FOR ADVERTISING DECISIONS

1. Leo Bogart, ''Is it Time to Discard the Audience Concept?'' *Journal of Marketing,* XXX (January, 1966), pp. 47-54, at p. 51.
2. Blaine Cooke, ''Is Advertising Important Enough in the Corporate Budget to Justify the Cost of Extensive Research?'' *Advertising Age* XXXVII (July 18, 1966), pp. 109-12, at p. 110.
3. See, for example, Herbert E. Krugman, ''Answering Some Unanswered Questions in Measuring Advertising Effectiveness,'' in *Proceedings,* 12th Annual Conference of the Advertising Research Foundation, October 5, 1966; or Kristian S. Palda, ''The Hypothesis of a Hierarchy of Effects: A Partial Evaluation,'' *Journal of Marketing Research,* III (February, 1966) pp. 13-24.
4. Steuart Henderson Britt, ''Advertising,'' *Encyclopedia Americana,* I (1967), pp. 195-206 at p. 195.
5. Patrick J. Robinson and David J. Luck, *Promotional Decision Making: Practice and Theory* (New York: McGraw-Hill Book Co., 1964).
6. Patrick J. Robinson (ed.), *Promotional Decisions Using Mathematical Models,* (Boston: Allyn and Bacon, Inc., 1967), pp. 43-85.
7. Alfred A. Kuehn and Albert C. Rohloff, ''Fitting Models To Aggregate Data.'' *Journal of Advertising Research,* VII (March, 1967), pp. 43-47, at p. 46.
8. See Neil H. Borden and Martin V. Marshall, *Advertising Management: Text and Cases* (Homewood, Ill.: Richard D. Irwin, Inc., 1959), Chapters II, III.
9. See, for example, James G. March and Herbert A. Simon, *Organizations* (New York: John Wiley and Sons, Inc., 1958), pp. 140-41.
10. Herbert D. Maneloveg, ''How Much Advertising is Enough?'' *Advertising Age,* XXXVII (June 6, 1966), pp. 130-32, at p. 130.
11. Patrick J. Robinson, ''Methodological Contributions to Advertising Strategy from Operations Research,'' *Michigan Advertising Papers,* No. 3 (Ann Arbor: Bureau of Business Research, School of Business Administration, University of Michigan, 1959), pp. 23-53.
12. Harry D. Wolfe *et al, Evaluating Media* (New York: National Industrial Conference Board, Studies in Business Policy No. 121, 1966).
13. Kristian S. Palda, *The Measurement of Cumulative Advertising Effects* (Englewood Cliffs, N.J.: Prentice-Hall, Inc., 1964).
14. Kurt H. Schaffir and Earle W. Orr, Jr., ''The Determination of Advertising Budgets for Brands,'' *Journal of Advertising Research,* III, (March, 1963), pp. 7-12 at p. 11.

15. See James E. Moyer, "Teflon, An Advertising Case History," (Available from du Pont Advertising Department); Raymond J. Jessen, "A Switch-Over Experimental Design to Measure Advertising Effect," *Journal of Advertising Research,* I (March, 1961) pp. 15-22; and James C. Becknell, Jr., and Robert W. McIsaac, "Test Marketing Cookware Coated with 'Teflon,' " *Journal of Advertising Research,* III (September, 1963), pp. 2 - 8.
16. Wendell F. Clement, Peter L. Henderson, and Cleveland P. Eley, *The Effect of Different Levels of Promotional Expenditures on Sales of Fluid Milk,* (Washington: U.S. Government Printing Office, 1965).
17. *Ibid.,* p. 5.
18. Patrick J. Robinson and David J. Luck, *Promotional Decision Making: Practice and Theory* (New York: McGraw-Hill Book Co., 1964) at p. 115.
19. *Ibid.*
20. *Ibid.,* pp. 26-27.
21. Charles K. Ramond, "Science in Wonderland," *Journal of Advertising Research,* I (September, 1960), p. 32.
22. Darrell Blaine Lucas and Steuart Henderson Britt, *Measuring Advertising Effectiveness* (New York: McGraw-Hill Book Company, Inc., 1963).

CHAPTER II. MEASURES OF PERFORMANCE

1. Robert J. Lavidge and Gary A. Steiner, "A Model for Predictive Measurements of Advertising Effectiveness," *Journal of Marketing,* XXV (October, 1961), pp. 59-62, at p. 61.
2. Russell H. Colley, *Defining Advertising Goals for Measured Advertising Results* (New York: Association of National Advertisers, 1961).

CHAPTER III. A FRAMEWORK FOR ANALYSIS

No footnotes.

CHAPTER IV. ASSUMPTIONS CONCERNING THE SCOPE OF ADVERTISING AND RESPONSE MEASURED

1. Joel N. Axelrod, "Reducing Advertising Failures by Concept Testing," *Journal of Marketing,* XXVIII (October, 1964), p. 41-44.
2. Darrell Blaine Lucas and Steuart Henderson Britt, *Measuring Advertising Effectiveness* (New York: McGraw-Hill Book Company, Inc., 1963), p. 176.
3. Harry D. Wolfe, James K. Brown, and G. Clark Thompson, *Measuring Advertising Results* (New York: National Industrial Conference Board, Studies in Business Policy, No. 102, 1962), p. 7.
4. Robert J. Lavidge and Gary A. Steiner, "A Model for Predictive Measurements of Advertising Effectiveness," *Journal of Marketing,* XXV (October, 1961), pp. 59-62, at p. 61.
5. Russell H. Colley, *Defining Advertising Goals for Measured Advertising Results* (New York: Association of National Advertisers, 1961), pp. 37-40.
6. Kristian S. Palda, "The Hypothesis of a Hierarchy of Effects: A Partial Evaluation," *Journal of Marketing Research,* III (February, 1966), pp. 13-24, at p. 13.
7. *Ibid.,* p. 14.
8. *Ibid.,* p. 23.

9. Joseph E. Bachelder, "DAGMAR's Legs," Proceedings, American Marketing Association, New York, June 14-16, 1965, pp. 349-53, at p. 351.

10. Seymour Smith, "DAGMAR – What's Wrong With Her Measurements?" Proceedings, American Marketing Association, New York, June 14-16, 1965, pp. 333-39, at p. 337.

11. Lee Adler, Allan Greenberg, and Darrell B. Lucas, "What Big Agency Men Think of Copy Testing Methods," *Journal of Marketing Research,* II (November, 1965), pp. 339-45.

12. Lucas and Britt, *op. cit.,* p. 101.

13. Adler, Greenberg, and Lucas, *op. cit.,* p. 345.

14. Raymond A. Bauer, "Attitudes, Variable Behavior, and Other Behavior," *Attitude Research at Sea,* ed. Lee Adler and Irving Crespi (Chicago: American Marketing Association, 1966), pp. 3-14, at p. 4.

15. Melvin L. DeFleur and Frank R. Westie, "Verbal Attitudes and Overt Act: An Experiment in the Salience of Attitudes," *American Psychological Review,* XXIII (December, 1958), pp. 667-73.

16. Leon Festinger, "Behavioral Support for Opinion Change," *Public Opinion Quarterly,* XXVIII (Fall, 1964), pp. 404-17, at p. 417.

17. See Charles K. Ramond, "Must We Communicate to Sell?" *Journal of Advertising Research,* IV (March, 1964), pp. 57-59, at p. 59.

18. Cornelius DuBois, "The Story of Brand XL: How Consumer Attitudes Its Market Position?" Proceedings of the Fifteenth Conference on Public Opinion Research. *Public Opinion Quarterly,* XXIV (Fall, 1960), pp. 480-81.

19. Valentine Appel, "Attitude Change: Another Dubious Method for Measuring Advertising Effectiveness," in Adler and Crespi, *op. cit.,* pp. 141-52, at p. 150.

20. Bernard Berelson and Gary A. Steiner, *Human Behavior and Inventory of Scientific Findings* (New York: Harcourt Brace Edward, 1964), pp. 103-04.

21. Herbert E. Krugman, "Some Applications of Pupil Measurement," *Journal of Marketing Research,* I (November, 1964), pp. 15-19, at p. 19.

22. Peter E. Nathan and Wallace H. Wallace, "An Operant Behavioral Measure of TV Commercial Effectiveness," *Journal of Advertising Research,* V (December, 1965), pp. 13-20.

23. Lucas and Britt, *op. cit.,* p. 157.

24. Dianne Z. Newman and Wallace H. Wallace, "Validation of an Operant Conditioning Technique Through Induced Sales Data," A Report to the Eastern Psychological Association (Boston, April 6-8, 1967), p. 5.

25. Palda, *op. cit.,* p. 13.

26. Adler, Greenberg and Lucas, *op. cit.,* p. 343.

27. *Ibid.*

28. *Ibid.,* p. 344.

29. Martin Mayer, *The Intelligent Man's Guide to Sales Measures of Advertising* (New York: Advertising Research Foundation, 1965) pp. 7-8.

30. Charles K. Ramond, "Must Advertising Communicate to Sell?" *Harvard Business Review,* XLIII (September-October, 1965), pp. 148-59, at p. 150.

31. Colley, *op. cit.,* p. 53.

32. Blaine Cooke, "Is Advertising Important Enough in the Corporate Budget to Justify the Cost of Extensive Research?" *Advertising Age* XXXVII (July 18, 1966) pp. 109-12, at p. 112. See also James M. Wallace, "A Perfect Measurment of Advertising's Contribution to Marketing," *Journal of Marketing,* XXX (July, 1966), p. 16.

CHAPTER V. ASSUMPTIONS CONCERNING THE
ENVIRONMENTAL FACTORS

1. Lee Adler, Allen Greenberg, and Darrell B. Lucas, "What Big Agency Men Think of Copy Testing Methods," *Journal of Marketing Research,* II (November, 1965), pp. 339-45, at p. 341.
2. Leo Bogart, "Is It Time to Discard the Audience Concept?" *Journal of Marketing,* XXX (January, 1966), pp. 47-54, at p. 51.
3. Richard H. Ostheimer, "Comparing the Influence of Media Context on Advertising," in *1965 Proceedings,* Business and Economic Statistics Section, American Statistical Association, pp. 236-42, at. p. 236.
4. Carl I. Hovland, Irving L. Janis and Harold H. Kelley, *Communication and Persuasion* (New Haven: Yale University Press, 1953), pp. 269-70.
5. Carl I. Hovland *et al., The Order of Presentation in Persuasion* (New Haven: Yale University Press, 1957).
6. Ostheimer, *op. cit.,* p. 242.

CHAPTER VI. APPLICATIONS OF IMP ON ANALYZING
MEASUREMENT TECHNIQUES

1. William S. Hoofnagle, "Experimental Designs in Measuring the Effectiveness of Promotion," *Journal of Marketing Research,* II (May, 1965), pp. 154-62, at p. 154.
2. Peter L. Henderson, James F. Hind, and Sidney E. Brown, "Sales Effects of Two Campaign Themes," *Journal of Advertising Research,* I (December, 1961), pp. 2-11, at p. 9.
3. Hoofnagle, *op. cit.,* p. 161.
4. Charles K. Ramond, "Must Advertising Communicate to Sell?" *Harvard Business Review,* XLIII (September-October, 1965), pp. 148-59, at p. 158.
5. Edward S. Hughes, "Measuring Advertising Effectiveness," A Report to the Association of National Advertisers' Second Advanced Advertising Management Seminar (Highland Park, Illinois, October 13-18, 1964).

Index

Absolute advertising effectiveness, 17-18, 90

Adnorms, 34

Advertising:
allowance for, 8
campaign:
assessing success from portion of, 52
components, 4-6
decision(s), 4-10, 22-23, 90-91
definition, 4
effectiveness:
absolute measure, 17-18, 90
criterion, 20-21, 39
definition, 6
directions for future research, 93
problems in measuring, 5, 13-16
purchase and nonpurchase measures, 66-69
relative, 12-13, 17-18, 21, 46, 49, 54, 79, 82, 84-86, 90, 92-93
effects, some typical, 18-20
expenditure (see also Cost, Decision making)
determining budget, 8, 21-23
research approaches to, 10-13
goals:
interpretation, 20, 78-79
and marketing goals, 58
measurement (see also Idealized Measurement Procedure, Measurement conditions, Measurement techniques)
feasibility of, 2-3, 82
rationale for, 1-2
research approaches, 8-13
at stages of development process, 9
message, research into, 8-9

purpose, 4, 68
scope (see also Media)
assumptions, 51-54
basic attribute, 38-39
AIDA hierarchy of consumer interest, 57
AIDCA hierarchy of consumer interest, 57
Aided recall, 28-30
Assumptions underlying advertising measurement techniques, 47-80
basis for acceptance, 48-50
in comparing advertising alternatives, 77-79
conditions of exposure, 71-74
conditions of measurement, 74-76
correlates of effects, 24
data handling, 79
how to evaluate, 82
response being measured, 51-70
sampling procedure, 76-77
scope of advertising, 51-54
with use of norm, 77-79
Attitude:
relation to purchasing behavior, 24, 61-63
response measure, 15, 29, 31, 33, 40, 56, 57-58, 61-63, 67
Attributes of measurement techniques, 37, 38-46
Audience Studies, Inc., 27-28, 42, 64
Awareness:
relation to purchase behavior, 56-58, 60-61
response measure, 31, 40, 56, 60-61, 67

Bias, 74-75
interviewee, 75

interviewer, 74-75
Buying attitude, 29, 30

Colley hierarchy approach, 21, 57,
    58-59
Commercial recognition (CR), 30
Commercial registration, proved
    (PCR), 30
Communication(s):
  as advertising function, 67-68
  goals, 58-59
  measures, 21, 24, 42, 67-70, 90
    evaluated by ad agency research
      directors, 59-60
    reliability v. ease of implemen-
      tation, 67-69
  research, findings from, 72-74
Comparative analysis:
  chart, 39
  procedure for selecting measure-
    ment techniques, 82-84
Comparison of alternatives:
  assumptions, 77-79
  basic attribute, 44-45
Competition, response to advertis-
  ing, 20
Component testing, 52
Concept testing, 52
Conditions   of   exposure,   41-42,
    71-74
Conditions of measurement, 42-43,
    74-76
Consumer panel study, 31-32
Consumer   responses,   18-19   (see
    also Response measures)
Context as dimension of measure-
    ment technique, 10, 41-42,
    71-74
Controlled   experiment(s),   11-13,
    30-31, 86-88
Correlates   of   effects,   23-25,   58,
    69, 70, 91
Cost:
  determination in relation to pro-
    fits, 45
  factor in technique choice, 21-22,
    81, 82-84
Coupons, 42

DAGMAR, 21, 57, 58-59, 69
Data handling:
  assumption of error in, 79
  basic attribute, 45
  in market tests, 88-89
Decision(s):
  advertising,   4-10,   22-23,   90-91

classifying, 5
definition, 4
marketing, 4-6, 22
media   selection   and   scheduling,
    10
Decision making:
  conditions necessary for, 48-49
  considerations in, 4, 18, 69-70
  criteria, 18-20, 90-91
  with   equal   cost   alternatives,
    21-25, 91
  ideal, 20
  summary, 90-91
  with   unequal   cost   alternatives,
    21-23, 25, 91
Differential weighting, 79

Editorial   environment   of   media,
    effect on response, 10, 41-42,
    71-74
Effectiveness   of   advertising   (see
    Advertising effectiveness)
Effects of advertising:
  on competitors, 20
  on consumers, 18-19
  on employees, 20
  on trade, 19
Electrical   conductivity   of   skin,
    64
Employees,   effect   of   advertising
    on, 20
Environmental   measurement   fac-
    tors, 10, 41-46, 71-80
Equal cost advertising alternatives,
    21-25, 90-91
Evaluation:
  of   alternative   techniques,   sum-
    mary, 91-92
  of assumptions, subjective, 81-82
  of test market procedure, 88-89
Experimental approach to advertis-
    ing   expenditure,   10,   11-13,
    86-88
  apple example, 87
  experimental design, 12, 86-88
  fluid milk example, 12
  Teflon example, 11-12
Exposure, conditions of:
  artificial, nonnatural, 72
  assumptions, 71-74
  basic attributes, 41-42
  editorial environment, 10, 41-42,
    72-74
  ideal, 41
  preferences of ad agency research
    directors, 71

Gallup and Robinson Magazine Impact Surveys, 28-29, 40, 61
Gallup and Robinson Total Prime Time, 29-30, 40, 45, 61
Goals, advertising and marketing, 20, 58, 78-79

Hierarchy of effects theory, 20-21, 39, 56-60
  AIDA formula, 57
  Colley approach, 21, 57, 58-59
  inadequacy, 21, 58-60, 90
  Lavidge and Steiner sequence, 57
  National Industrial Board concept, 56
Historical data analysis approach, 10-11, 13

Idea registration, 29, 30
Ideal sample, 43
Idealized Measurement Procedure (IMP):
  application in analyzing techniques, 1-2, 26-27, 81-89
  assumptions, 47-80
  comparative analysis with actual measurement techniques, 26-46
  and current practice, 47-48
  flexibility, 91-92
  guide for future research and development, 93
  steps in utilizing, 82-84, 91-92
Impact, of editorial context, 10, 41-42, 72-74
Inquiry, relation to sales, 55-56
Internal response measures, 40-41, 63-64, 65

Judgment, advertising, 7, 14, 15
  in choosing techniques, 54, 82, 84
  in evaluating assumptions, 48-49, 92

Knowledge of product:
  relation to purchase behavior, 58, 61
  response measure, 40, 57

Latin-square design, 12, 86
Lavidge and Steiner hierarchy sequence, 57
Life, 5, 73-74, 76

Look, 5, 73

McCall's, 73
Magazine readership studies, 28-29, 30-31, 40, 41, 43, 61, 72-74, 77
MAPP, 9
Marder Ad Evaluation Program, 30-31, 40, 41, 43, 44, 77
Market tests:
  applicability, 52, 86
  evaluation of procedure, 88-89
  nonsyndicated technique, 34-35
  for validation, 86-88
Marketing decisions, 4, 22
Marketing search actions, 55-56
Measurement (see also Advertising, Idealized Measurement Procedure, Response measures)
  conditions of:
    assumptions, 74-76
    basic attributes, 42-43
    biases introduced, 74-75
  techniques (see also Cost, Decision making, Judgment)
    actual compared with ideal, 27
    assumptions associated with, 47-80
    basic attributes, 38-46
    comparative analysis chart, 39
    dimensions, 46
    evaluated by ad agency research directors, 59, 66-67
    experimental design, 12, 86-88
    nonsyndicated, 34-37
    research approaches, 10-13
    selection, 82-84
    syndicated, 27-34
    validation, 49-50, 84-89
Media:
  audience composition and reach, 9-10
  context effects, 10, 41-42, 71-74
  element of advertising, 4, 38, 51-54
  inter-media considerations, 53
  intra-media considerations, 53
  research, 8-9, 53, 73-74
  selection and scheduling, 5, 9-10
Message research, 8-9
Milwaukee Advertising Laboratory, 31-32, 38, 45
Milwaukee Journal, 32

National Industrial Conference Board, 10, 56

New York Times, 72
Newspaper study, 32, 72-73
Nonexperimental approach to advertising expenditure, 10-11, 13
Nonpurchase measures of effectiveness, 39-41, 55-69 *(see also* Communication measures)
Nonsyndicated measurement techniques, 34-37
Nonverbal responses, 19 *(see also* Response measures)
Norms, 44-45, 78

Parade, 73
Physical responses:
  measure of, 40, 41, 42, 55
  relation to purchase behavior, 64-65
Physiological responses:
  measure of, 28, 36, 40-41, 42, 55
  relation to purchase behavior, 63-64, 65
Post-testing:
  controlled experiment, 28, 29, 33, 41, 78
  evaluation, 15
  hierarchy approach, 21
  historical data campaign, 66
  magazine impact surveys, 29, 78
  and number of inquiries, 55
  television, 28, 33
  time of, 9
  types, 10
Predisposition, 61-62 *(see also* Attitude)
Preference as response measure, 28, 33, 36, 40, 56
Pretesting:
  comparing alternatives, 44
  controlled experiment, 23, 24, 28, 29, 33, 41, 66, 78
  evaluation, 15
  hierarchy approach, 21
  magazine impact surveys, 29, 78
  and number of inquiries, 55
  television, 28, 33, 78
  time, 9
  types, 10
  unnatural context, 72
Product knowledge:
  relation to purchase behavior, 61
  response measures, 40, 57
Profits as criterion of effectiveness, 20-21, 23, 45, 66, 70, 90, 92 *(see also* Sales as criterion)

Proved commerical registration (PCR), 30
Proved name registration (PNR), 29
Psychogalvanometer:
  nonsyndicated measurement technique, 36
  validity for advertising research, 36, 65, 75
Psychometric scaling, 9
Publication readership tests, 36-37
Pupil variation (eye response), 64
Purchase measures of advertising effectiveness, 39-40, 54-55, 66-69, 85

Rank correlation, 23, 49
Reach of specific medium vehicle, 10
Recall:
  relation to purchase behavior, 67
  response measure, 28-30, 40, 56, 58, 61, 67
Recognition:
  relation to purchase behavior, 61
  response measure, 33-34, 60
Relative advertising effectiveness:
  criterion, 21
  meaning, 17-18, 46, 79, 92-93
  measured against IMP, 49, 54
  procedure in determining, 12-13, 82, 84-86, 90
Reliability:
  of communications measures, 68
  of measurement techniques, 48-49
  in sampling, 77
Research directors, advertising agency:
  evaluation of measurement techniques, 59-60, 66-67
  preferences in exposure conditions, 71
Response measures *(see also* specific services and techniques)
  assumptions, 54-70
  basic attributes, 39-41
  evaluated by ad agency research directors, 59-60, 66-67
  ideal unit, 39, 42
  internal (physiological), 29, 36, 40-41, 42, 55, 63-64, 65
  marketing search, 55-56
  nonpurchase, 39-41, 55-70
  physical, 40, 41, 42, 55, 64-65
  purchase, 39, 54-55, 66-69

typical, 18-20
verbal, 19, 39, 56-63
weighting, 79

Sales as criterion of effectiveness,
     11-13, 66-69, 85, 86-88
Salivation, 64
Sampling:
  assumptions, 76-77
  basic attribute, 43-44
  nonparticipation, 76-77
  nonprobability, 77
  probability, 77
  restrictions, 43-44, 76-77
  size, 43, 44, 77
Saturday Evening Post, 30-31, 43,
     76
Schwerin Standard TV Testing Ser-
     vice, 32-33, 40, 44, 78
Scope of advertising *(see also*
     Media)
  assumptions, 51-54
  basic attributes, 38-39
Secondary standards, 85-86, 89
Simulated purchase, 39-40
Sleeper effect, 53
Split-run test, 36-37, 38, 55, 77
Starch Readership Service, 33-34,
     38, 40, 55, 61, 78
Syndicated measurement services,
     9, 14, 27-34 *(see also* specific
     names)

Teflon advertising example, 11-12
Television test, on-air, 35-36
Television testing services, 27-28,
     29-30, 32-33, 35-36
This Week, 32, 73
Timing, factor in technique choice,
     81
Trade, effect of advertising on, 19
True, 72

Unaided recall, 36, 61
Unequal cost advertising decisions,
     21-23, 25, 91
U.S. Department of Agriculture,
     86-87

Validity:
  of attitudinal responses, 62-63
  of intermediate responses, 57-58
  of measurement techniques,
     13-16, 49-50, 81-82, 84-89

of psychogalvanometer in adver-
     tising research, 36, 65
of recognition method, 61
of single v. multiple insertions,
     53
Verbal responses:
  evaluation by research directors,
     59-60, 66-67
  measurement of consumer inter-
     est, 19, 39, 56-63